HOMEWORK
SURVIVAL GUIDE

American History

A REFERENCE FOR STUDENTS AND PARENTS

by Susan Kantor

illustrated by Andrea Champlin

Copyright © 1999 by Troll Communications L.L.C.

Cover and interior pages designed by: Bob Filipowich

Developed and produced by: WWK Consulting Group, Inc., 201 West 70 Street, New York, NY 10023

We gratefully acknowledge The Library of Congress for permission to reprint photographs on pages 18, 37, 46, 47, 52, and 55.

We have made every effort to trace the holders of the photographs and documents used in this book. If for any reason there have been any omissions, we will be happy to acknowledge them in future printings.

Printed in the United States of America. ISBN 0-8167-5525-6
10 9 8 7 6 5 4 3 2

● ●

Helping children do their homework successfully requires some planning. Study habits and time management are important skills for children to learn. The following tips may give you and your child strategies for doing homework more efficiently. Both you and your child will learn to survive American History homework!

- Have your child do homework immediately after coming home from school. A quick snack is okay, but any other activity should wait until later.

- Make sure your child has a quiet, well-lit place to work.

- Help your child gather the materials necessary for his or her homework. Remember to have enough pencils, paper, and other tools ready.

- Try to schedule after-school activities on days when there is not as much homework.

- Long-term projects take planning. Encourage your child to work on a lengthy project in small sections, rather than tackling it all in one evening.

- Children need encouragement and reassurance. Patience and praise help children become better students.

- Encourage your child to read the newspaper and news magazines. These resources help children learn to appreciate a broad sense of history.

● ●

CHAPTER 1

America's Earliest Days

THE FIRST AMERICANS

About twenty thousand years ago, hunters following their prey walked across a **land bridge** from northeast Asia to Alaska. Because Alaska is located on the continent of North America, these hunters are called the first Americans. Their descendants are the people now known as **Native Americans**.

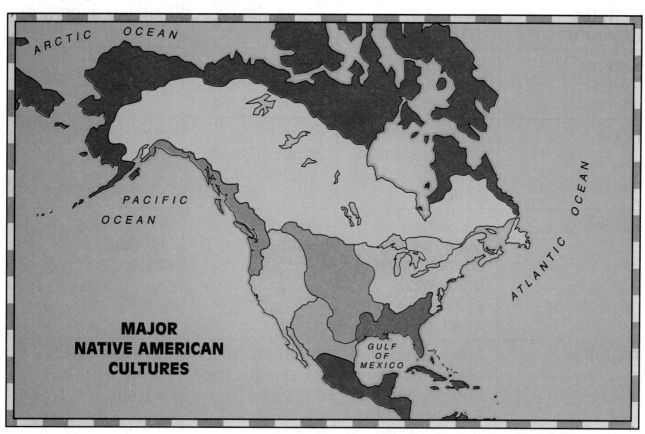

MAJOR NATIVE AMERICAN CULTURES

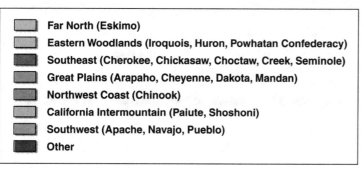

Far North (Eskimo)

Eastern Woodlands (Iroquois, Huron, Powhatan Confederacy)

Southeast (Cherokee, Chickasaw, Choctaw, Creek, Seminole)

Great Plains (Arapaho, Cheyenne, Dakota, Mandan)

Northwest Coast (Chinook)

California Intermountain (Paiute, Shoshoni)

Southwest (Apache, Navajo, Pueblo)

Other

THE FIRST AMERICANS

By the time European explorers came to America, millions of Native Americans were already living throughout North and South America. They belonged to many different culture groups, or **tribes**. Each tribe developed its own traditions and way of life. The chart below highlights some differences among tribes in three very different regions.

THREE NATIVE AMERICAN CULTURES

	Chinook (Northwest Coast)	Eskimo (Far North)	Pueblo (Southwest)
Climate/ Environment	mild, rainy; dense forests	very cold; frozen seas	hot, dry desert
Shelter	wooden plank houses made from cedar trees	animal skin tents/igloos of snow and ice	adobe houses
Food	clams, oysters, shrimp, salmon; deer, moose, bear	polar bears, caribou, seals, whales, walrus	corn, beans, squash
Clothing	elk skins, cedar-bark coats; copper bracelets; elaborate headdresses	seal and caribou skin	loose-fitting, light cotton clothing
Religion	honored spirits of animals they hunted; carved totem poles to record history of their families	honored spirits of animals they hunted	honored spirits of nature
Transportation	canoes	kayaks for fishing/hunting	none

In 1001, a group of Northern Europeans called Vikings, led by **Leif Eriksson**, sailed from Greenland, which is a very large island near the North Pole, to Newfoundland—off the east coast of North America. They established the colony of **Vinland** (meaning fertile region).

Almost five hundred years later, in 1492, **Christopher Columbus** reached America, but he landed off the southern coast of North America, on San Salvador Island in the Bahamas. Columbus mistakenly thought he had reached the East Indian islands (off the coast of Asia), so he named the dark-skinned natives **"Indians"**— but they were actually one of the Native American tribes. At this time, about ten million Native Americans lived in North America.

America is named for **Amerigo Vespucci**, an Italian merchant and mapmaker who explored the New World for Spain and Portugal. Vespucci figured out that the land Columbus explored was not part of Asia. He realized it was a different continent.

Who were the first Americans and where did they come from? Write your answer on the flap.

EARLY EUROPEAN EXPLORERS OF THE NEW WORLD

Explorers	Explored for	Major Discoveries
Leif Eriksson	Vikings (Norway)	Newfoundland (1001)
Christopher Columbus	Spain	San Salvador and West Indies (1492)
Amerigo Vespucci	Spain, Portugal	South America (1499)
Vasco de Balboa	Spain	Pacific Ocean (1513)
Juan Ponce de León	Spain	Florida (1513)
Hernando Cortés	Spain	Aztecs of Mexico (1519)
Giovanni da Verrazano	France	Eastern coast of North America (1524)
Francisco Pizarro	Spain	Incas of Peru (1531)
Jacques Cartier	France	St. Lawrence River (1534)
Francisco de Coronado	Spain	Grand Canyon (1540)
Hernando de Soto	Spain	Mississippi River (1541)
Juan Rodriguez Cabrillo	Spain	California (1542)
Samuel de Champlain	France	The Great Lakes (1603)
Henry Hudson	Netherlands	Hudson River (1609)

OVERSEAS EXPLORATION

Exploring new lands was expensive. Powerful nation-states (Portugal, Spain, France, and England) financed overseas exploration in hopes of getting rich through trade. Other reasons for exploration during this period of history include:

- Bigger and faster ships were becoming available.
- Navigational devices, such as the astrolabe (used to determine position at sea), quadrant, compass, and sextant, were invented.
- Many people have always had a strong desire to explore the unknown.

INLAND EXPLORATION

Several famous explorers worked for France. **Jacques Marquette** was a French missionary who traveled to Canada to convert Native Americans to Christianity. **Louis Jolliet** was born in Canada. He knew many Native American languages and was a skilled explorer. In 1673, the governor of **New France** (the territory claimed by French explorers, which included land from Canada to the Gulf of Mexico) asked Marquette and Jolliet to explore the Mississippi River. Marquette kept a detailed journal of their travels.

René-Robert La Salle, a French fur trader, lived in Canada. In 1682, he and a group of Frenchmen and Native Americans explored the Mississippi River. All the land drained by the river was claimed by La Salle for **Louis XIV**, king of France. La Salle named the region Louisiana in honor of the king.

Who discovered the Pacific Ocean? Write your answer on the flap.

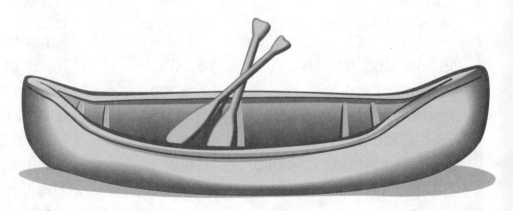

Birch-bark Canoe

A **colony** is a settlement far from the **colonists'** home country. In 1584, **Queen Elizabeth I** of England gave **Sir Walter Raleigh** a **charter** (official royal permission) to establish an English colony in North America. Raleigh chose land near the outer bank of North Carolina. He named it **Virginia** in honor of Elizabeth, who was known as the Virgin Queen.

In 1585, Raleigh started the colony of **Roanoke**, but the colonists were discouraged by shortages of food and supplies and soon returned to England. In 1587, more colonists arrived to settle in Roanoke, but three years later another group of English settlers found the colony deserted. Because the colonists' disappearance remains a mystery, Roanoke is called the **Lost Colony**.

Unlike Roanoke, the colony of **Jamestown** succeeded, thanks to John Smith. In 1607, he was part of an expedition—financed by the **Virginia Company** of London—that founded Jamestown. It was the first permanent colony in the New World. In 1608, Smith became leader of Jamestown. The colony was failing, and the sick and starving colonists wanted to return to England. Under Smith's strict leadership, however, conditions began to improve.

The colony of Jamestown survived for the following reasons:

- **representative government**, set up by the Virginia Company

- the growth and profitable sale in England of tobacco—a Native American crop

- trade with Native Americans

- a lengthy period of peace brought about when Chief Powhatan's daughter **Pocahontas** married **John Rolfe**, a settler

About ten years later, another type of colony was established farther north by a group of 102 **Pilgrims** (people who make a journey for religious reasons). In September of 1620, they left England on the *Mayflower* and set sail for Virginia. Blown off course, they landed at a harbor near Cape Cod, Massachusetts. They named the spot **Plymouth** after a town in England.

Because Plymouth was located outside the region controlled by the Virginia Company, it had no government to make or enforce laws. The Pilgrims didn't believe that government should be unnecessarily powerful, but they were used to following laws and knew that without them people might be too self-serving.

In a representative government, citizens elect their leaders. In Jamestown, the elected officials were called burgesses. The first session of the House of Burgesses met in 1619. It was their job to suggest laws. This form of government became the model for all later English colonies.

What type of government did Jamestown have? Write your answer on the flap.

Who was given a charter to establish the first English colony in North America? Write your answer on the flap.

Before leaving the ship, therefore, Pilgrim leaders wrote an agreement called the **Mayflower Compact**. By signing it, the Pilgrims promised to follow any "just and equal" laws that would be made for the welfare of the new colony.

By the mid 1700s, thirteen permanent colonies were thriving along the east coast of America.

THE THIRTEEN ORIGINAL COLONIES

First Permanent Settlement Founded	Leaders	Religion
NEW ENGLAND		
Massachusetts		
Plymouth/1620 (became part of the Massachusetts Bay Colony in 1691)	William Bradford	Puritan
Massachusetts Bay/1630	John Winthrop	Puritan
New Hampshire/1623	Colonists from Massachusetts	Protestant
Rhode Island/1636	Roger Williams	Religious freedom
Connecticut/1633	Thomas Hooker	Protestant
MIDDLE COLONIES		
New York/1624	Peter Minuit	Dutch Reformed
Delaware/1638	William Penn	Quaker
New Jersey/1660	John Berkeley, George Carteret	Quaker, Dutch Reformed
Pennsylvania/1643	William Penn	Quaker
SOUTHERN		
Virginia/1607	John Smith	Anglican
Maryland/1634	Lord Baltimore	Catholic, Protestant
Carolina Territory/1663 (split into North and South Carolina in 1712)	Group of Eight Proprietors*	Protestant
Georgia/1733	James Oglethorpe	Baptist

*People given land in the New World by the King of England were known as **proprietors.** They were allowed to divide the land and rent it to others but were required to make a yearly payment to the king.

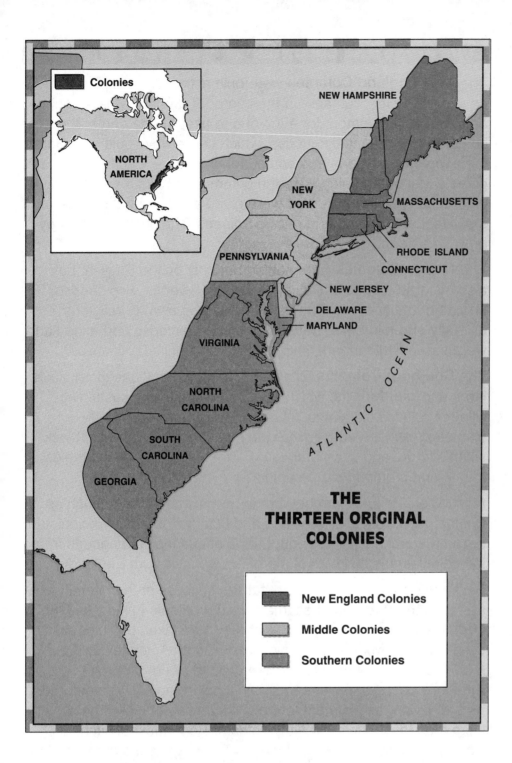

Colonies

NORTH AMERICA

NEW HAMPSHIRE

NEW YORK

MASSACHUSETTS

RHODE ISLAND
CONNECTICUT

PENNSYLVANIA

NEW JERSEY

DELAWARE
MARYLAND

VIRGINIA

NORTH CAROLINA

SOUTH CAROLINA

GEORGIA

ATLANTIC OCEAN

THE THIRTEEN ORIGINAL COLONIES

New England Colonies

Middle Colonies

Southern Colonies

How many colonies did William Penn lead? Write your answer on the flap.

DIVERSE RELIGIONS

Among the colonists who established the various colonies there were several different religions. Members of the Church of England were known as Anglicans. Pilgrims were first called Separatists because they had separated from the Church of England. Puritans did not want to separate from the Church of England but did want to change and "purify" it. They became known as Protestants. Pilgrims and Baptists grew out of the Puritan movement.

Name the four
Middle Colonies.
Write your answer
on the flap.

COMPARING THE COLONIES

The **New England Colonies** were built according to a plan developed by the Puritans. In the center of a village was an open area, called a common, for everyone to use. At one end of the common was the meetinghouse, which was always built first. Here, the people worshipped and settled town matters. Each family was given a plot of land alongside the common to build a home and plant a garden. Families also were given strips of land outside of the village for farming and raising animals. The surplus food they grew was traded for goods.

The **Middle Colonies** were settled not only by the English, but also by large groups of Dutch, Germans, Swedes, Scotch-Irish, and other nationalities. The colonies were known for religious diversity and tolerance. Settlers worked in factories and mines and were successful farmers, shipbuilders, and skilled artisans.

The **Southern Colonies** established an economy based on slave labor and **plantations**, which resembled small, self-sustaining villages. Slaves did almost all of the work. Surrounding the plantation owner's house were the smokehouse, flour mill, black-smith's forge, and sewing house. Farther away were the stables, barns, and cramped slave cabins.

Most colonists were farmers, but in towns with harbors (such as Boston, New York, Philadelphia, and Charleston), many colonists became merchants. They bought and sold agricultural goods from the colonies and all kinds of merchandise sent from England.

Because slaves were important for the success of the plantation system, the slave trade became a very profitable business. **The Middle Passage** was the name of the route taken by ships that carried slaves from Africa to North and South America. By the 1700s, about one hundred thousand slaves were brought to the Americas each year. Guns or small sums of money were offered for each slave as payment to their African captors, and the slaves were then loaded into the filthy holds of Portuguese, Dutch, Spanish, English, and French ships. To escape a life of certain misery, many slaves refused to eat or threw themselves into the ocean. Chained together, with rarely enough room to sit up, thousands died on this horrible journey every year.

The trade conducted along the triangle-shaped route from the thirteen English colonies to the West Indies to Africa was known as **Triangular Trade**. Slaves, molasses, and rum were bought and sold along the three legs of the journey.

CHAPTER 2

From Colonists to Free Citizens

● ●

It took a lot of effort, but the colonies finally separated from their powerful nation-states—the countries that had originally financed the exploration of the New World.

FRENCH AND INDIAN WAR (1754–1763)

In the **French and Indian War**, which began in 1754 and was fought between the French and the British, most Native American (or "Indian") tribes sided with the French against the British and the colonists. The Indians feared that if the colonists won the war, they would take even more Indian land.

The French won most of the battles until 1757, when **William Pitt** took charge of Great Britain's war plans. Pitt was able to get all the money, troops, and supplies he needed to win the war.

Causes of the War:

- France and Great Britain both want to control the Ohio River Valley.

- France begins to build forts near Lake Erie, intruding on English territory.

- The governor of Virginia sends **George Washington** to warn the French that there will be a war if they do not stop building forts and return to Canada. The French refuse.

- In 1754, Washington is sent to attack the French at **Fort Duquesne** in present-day Pennsylvania.

- Without enough soldiers or weapons for the attack, Washington sets up a crude fort, **Fort Necessity**, to await help.

- Before help can arrive, the French and their Native American allies attack Fort Necessity. Outnumbered, Washington retreats. This battle marks the beginning of the French and Indian War.

Results of the War:

- The British and the colonists win the war. The **Treaty of Paris** is signed in 1763.

- The British gain control of Canada.
- The British gain French territories east of the Mississippi River (Spain gets New Orleans).
- The British receive Florida from Spain.
- The Mississippi Valley is opened to westward expansion.
- The main language and culture in North America becomes English rather than French.

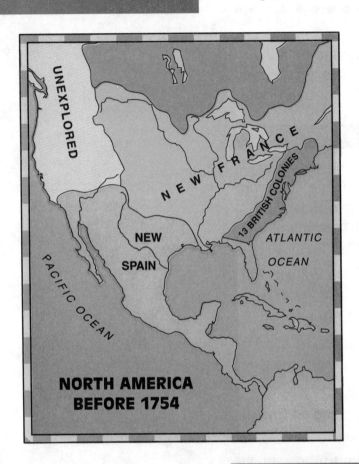

NORTH AMERICA BEFORE 1754

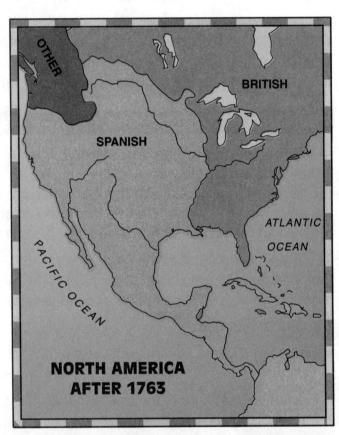

NORTH AMERICA AFTER 1763

AMERICAN REVOLUTION (1775–1783)

Britain's attempt to tax the colonists to help pay for the French and Indian War was one of the main causes of the **American Revolution**. The spirit of the revolution is portrayed in "Concord Hymn," written by the American poet Ralph Waldo Emerson. It was sung at the completion of the Concord Monument on July 4, 1837, and commemorates the battle in Lexington, Massachusetts, that marks the formal beginning of the Revolutionary War on April 19, 1775. The hymn begins with these famous lines:

> *By the rude bridge that arched the flood,*
> *Their flag to April's breeze unfurled,*
> *Here once the embattled farmers stood*
> *And fired the shot heard round the world.*

Events Leading to Revolution:

1763: In hopes of keeping peace with the Native Americans, the British Parliament issues the **Proclamation of 1763** calling for colonists not to settle west of the Appalachian Mountains and for those already there "to remove themselves" at once. Britain sends ten thousand troops to the colonies to enforce this law, but many colonists simply ignore it and move west anyway.

1765: Parliament passes the **Stamp Act**—a tax on all types of documents. The colonists believe that since they have no representation in Parliament, they should not have to pay taxes passed by Parliament. The colonists call these taxes "taxation without representation."

1770: Five colonists are killed when British soldiers fire into a noisy crowd. Patriot leader **Samuel Adams** calls the incident the **Boston Massacre**.

1773: Colonists object to a tax on tea called the **Tea Act**. Disguised as Mohawk Indians, they board ships carrying tea in Boston Harbor and throw the shipments overboard. The protest is called the **Boston Tea Party**.

1774: As punishment, Boston Harbor is closed and town meetings are forbidden. Colonists are also required to house and feed five thousand British troops sent to the colonies to assure that discipline is enforced. Colonists say these conditions cannot be allowed or tolerated. They call the laws the **Intolerable Acts**.

1774: Colonial leaders arrange a meeting in Philadelphia (the **First Continental Congress**) to decide a response to the Intolerable Acts. They send a letter of protest to the king, boycott British goods, begin to train soldiers, and gather war supplies.

1775: **Minutemen** (colonial army volunteers) confront British soldiers at **Lexington** and **Concord**, when the so-called shot heard round the world marks the beginning of the American Revolution.

1775: Delegates to the **Second Continental Congress** agree to form a **Continental Army**. George Washington is appointed commander-in-chief.

AMERICAN REVOLUTION

The Townshend Acts (1767) taxed items that were imported to the colonies. The colonists refused to purchase these goods. In 1770 the tax was lifted on everything except for tea.

A Minuteman

Colonists chose sides. Those who remained loyal to Great Britain and King George were called Loyalists. Those in favor of independence called themselves Patriots.

AMERICAN REVOLUTION

Independent and a New Nation:

1776: Members of the Second Continental Congress vote for independence from Great Britain. A committee is appointed to write the **Declaration of Independence**. Included are **Thomas Jefferson**, **Benjamin Franklin**, **John Adams**, **Roger Sherman**, and **Robert Livingston**. The Declaration of Independence is the most important document in American history. It expresses the standards by which Americans try to live and the values that form a common bond among all the citizens in the country.

1781: When Washington defeats British **General Charles Cornwallis** at the Battle of Yorktown in Virginia, the colonists win the war—and are, therefore, no longer colonists but citizens of the new American union of states. The country wasn't officially called the United States of America until the **Constitutional Convention** met in 1787.

1783: The **Treaty of Paris** is signed in Paris. America is recognized as an independent nation.

Results of the Revolution:

- Great Britain gives up all claims to owning land in the new union of states.
- Borders of the new nation reach from the Atlantic Ocean to the Mississippi River and from Canada to the top part of Florida (Spain controls most of Florida).
- Great Britain keeps Canada.

Delegates to the Continental Congress in 1776 accepted the Declaration of Independence on July 4, which has been celebrated ever since as Independence Day.

THE DECLARATION OF INDEPENDENCE

The Preamble

When in the Course of human events, it becomes necessary for one people to dissolve the political bands which have connected them with another, and to assume among the Powers of the earth, the separate and equal station to which the Laws of Nature and of Nature's God entitle them, a decent respect to the opinions of mankind requires that they should declare the causes which impel them to the separation.

A Declaration of Rights

We hold these truths to be self-evident, that all men are created equal, that they are endowed by their Creator with certain unalienable Rights, that among these are Life, Liberty, and the pursuit of Happiness.

That to secure these rights, Governments are instituted among Men, deriving their just powers from the consent of the governed.

The complete text of the Declaration of Independence can be summarized as follows:

- **The Preamble** explains why the Declaration of Independence was written.

- **Part 1** (A Declaration of Rights) is an explanation of the basic rights and principles on which the nation was founded—that all men are created equal and are entitled to "life, liberty, and the pursuit of happiness."

- **Part 2** (A Bill of Indictment) offers a lengthy list of grievances against **King George III**.

- **Part 3** (A Statement of Independence) states that "these United Colonies are, and of right ought to be, free and independent states . . ." and that all ties with Britain are now broken.

REVOLUTIONARY PERSONALITIES

Abigail Adams wrote to her husband, **John Adams**, when he was helping prepare the Declaration of Independence: "If . . . attention is not paid to the ladies, we are determined to stir up a rebellion and will not regard ourselves as bound by any laws in which we have had no voice or representation."

Benedict Arnold had been one of George Washington's most trusted generals. But Arnold betrayed his country when he arranged to turn over a fort at West Point under his command to the British in exchange for money.

Benjamin Franklin was a scientist, inventor (bifocal glasses, the Franklin stove), writer (*Poor Richard's Almanac*), and diplomat. In Philadelphia, he reformed the police force, organized a fire department, set up the first lending library, and helped start an academy that became the University of Pennsylvania.

When the brave patriot **Nathan Hale** was hanged by the British as a spy, his last words were: "I only regret that I have but one life to lose for my country."

Patrick Henry, a member of the House of Burgesses and five-time governor of Virginia, believed Great Britain had no right to tax the colonists. In defending the rights of the colonists, he demanded: "I know not what course others may take, but as for me, give me liberty or give me death."

In George Washington's first cabinet, **Thomas Jefferson** was Secretary of State and **Alexander Hamilton** was Secretary of the Treasury. They later formed the first political parties. Jefferson, a **Democratic-Republican**, believed in a strong state government. Hamilton, a **Federalist**, believed in a strong federal government.

A committee was appointed to write the Declaration of Independence. List as many committee members as you can on the flap.

Who founded the Federalist party? Write your answer on the flap.

When a British captain asked **John Paul Jones** if he was ready to surrender his sinking ship, the determined Jones replied: "I have not yet begun to fight!"

The French were the colonists' most important foreign allies. A French nobleman and officer, the **Marquis de Lafayette**, fought with George Washington at Brandywine, spent the winter with the Continental Army in Valley Forge, and led many raids against the British.

Thomas Paine hated governments that are based on inherited privilege. He was a philosopher, a writer, and the publisher of *Common Sense*—a widely read pamphlet that promoted American independence.

Paul Revere raced on horseback from Boston to Concord, warning colonists along the way that the British were coming. The British, also called **redcoats** because of the red jackets they wore, planned to capture arms and ammunition the colonists had hidden at Concord.

After the Revolution, **George Washington** encouraged the states to form a strong national government. Greatly admired for his leadership skills and devotion to duty, Washington was elected the first president of the new nation in 1789. After leaving office, he retired to Mount Vernon, his home in Virginia.

Thomas Jefferson

George Washington

Abigail Adams

John Adams

CHAPTER 3

Creating a Government

After the American Revolution, delegates from each state met in Philadelphia. They wanted a government strong enough to hold the states together, but not so powerful that individuals would lose their rights. In 1777, a **constitution**, or set of laws and principles for a national government, was written. It was called the **Articles of Confederation** and stated that the national government would have only powers given to it by the states. A law-making body, or **Congress**, was set up. In Congress, each state—no matter its size or population—had one vote. The constitution of 1777 had some problems. About ten years after it was written, a tax protest called **Shays' Rebellion** revealed the document's weaknesses.

SHAYS' REBELLION

In Massachusetts, farmers had a hard time paying their taxes after the Revolutionary War. Many of them wound up losing their land. **Daniel Shays**, a former captain in the army, gathered almost two thousand men to protest the situation. On January 25, 1787, they attempted to take over the federal arsenal in Springfield. Since there was no national army to stop them, the state militia had to put down the revolt. Shays' Rebellion made the nation's leaders realize that the Articles of Confederation did not provide for a government that was strong enough to protect the country. Another set of laws had to be created.

THE U.S. CONSTITUTION

Delegates to the Constitutional Convention met in Philadelphia in 1787 to write a new constitution. The scholarly **James Madison**, of Virginia, was considered the best-prepared delegate. Madison presented a plan for a constitution to replace the Articles of Confederation. This plan called for a strong national government with three branches: **executive**, **legislative**, and **judicial**. After much debate and many compromises, the delegates agreed on the new constitution. Because no one branch of government had complete power, the personal freedom of the people was protected.

James Madison is known as the "Father of the Constitution."

THE U.S. CONSTITUTION

The introduction to the Constitution is called the **preamble**.

PREAMBLE TO THE CONSTITUTION

We the people of the United States, in order to form a more perfect union, establish justice, insure domestic tranquility, provide for the common defense, promote the general welfare, and secure the blessings of liberty to ourselves and our posterity, do ordain and establish this Constitution for the United States of America.

The constitution that was written in 1787 is still honored in the United States today. Here is a brief explanation of the goals stated in the U.S. Constitution:

- **"form a more perfect union"**—national government was given the powers it needs to unify and strengthen the country;
- **"establish justice"**—a national court system was created;
- **"insure domestic tranquility"**—police agencies were formed to protect life and property;
- **"provide for the common defense"**—the value of a national military power was acknowledged;
- **"promote the general welfare"**— government programs for education and health could be created;
- **"secure the blessings of liberty"**—American citizens were now free to live as they pleased as long as they obeyed the law.

In addition to the specific goals stated in the U.S. Constitution, the following principles helped shape its theoretical foundation:

- **popular sovereignty**—people rule by voting;
- **limited government**—government must answer to the people;
- **federalism**—power is divided between national and state governments;
- **separation of powers**—powers and responsibilities are divided among three branches of government;
- **checks and balances**—each branch of the government has the power to check, or control, the authority of the other two branches.

In 1777, a constitution for a new national government was written. What was it called? Write your answer on the flap.

What are the three branches of the U.S. government? Write your answer on the flap.

One of the U.S. Constitution's many strong points is that it can be amended, or changed, as the country grows and changes. The first ten amendments of the Constitution protect the rights of individual citizens. These ten amendments are known as the **Bill of Rights**. The **first amendment** guarantees each United States citizen the freedoms of speech, press, religion, assembly, and petition.

CHECKS AND BALANCES IN U.S. GOVERNMENT

Branch of Government	Power	Checks
Legislative	Congress, made up of the Senate and the House of Representatives, passes laws. It has the power to tax, to coin money, and to declare war.	**Checks on Executive** • can override president's veto • can impeach president • confirms executive appointments and treaties **Checks on Judicial** • creates lower federal courts • can impeach judges • approves appointments of federal judges • can propose amendments to overrule judicial decisions
Executive	The president is the chief executive of the country. He enforces federal laws, makes political appointments, negotiates foreign treaties, and sends the annual budget to Congress for approval.	**Checks on Legislative** • can propose and veto bills • can call special sessions of Congress **Checks on Judicial** • appoints federal judges • can grant pardons to federal offenders
Judicial	The Supreme Court was created by the Judiciary Act of 1789. Its main business is to explain and interpret laws.	**Checks on Executive** • can declare executive actions unconstitutional **Checks on Legislative** • can declare acts of Congress unconstitutional

ORDER OF POWER IN THE U.S. GOVERNMENT

Which branch of the U.S. government passes laws? Write your answer on the flap.

WASHINGTON, D.C., OUR NATION'S CAPITAL

In 1783, Congress met in Philadelphia to discuss the need for a new and permanent national capital. The Residence Act, passed by Congress in 1790, provided for a 10-mile (16-km) square-shaped area for a new capital to be situated on the Potomac River. George Washington chose the site, which was named the District of Columbia (in honor of Christopher Columbus). He appointed a French architect, Pierre L'Enfant, to design the city, and he supervised the construction. Washington, D.C., became the capital in 1800. Originally called Federal City, it was renamed by Congress for the country's first president. Many of the major sights of the city are located on the Mall. This open, grassy area runs from the Capitol Building, which houses the United States Congress, all the way to the Potomac River.

ORDER OF POWER IN THE U.S. GOVERNMENT

If the president is unable to perform his duties, the following is the order in which power is assumed:

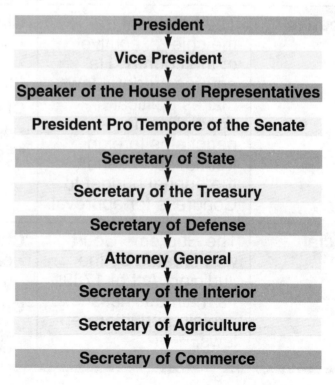

President
↓
Vice President
↓
Speaker of the House of Representatives
↓
President Pro Tempore of the Senate
↓
Secretary of State
↓
Secretary of the Treasury
↓
Secretary of Defense
↓
Attorney General
↓
Secretary of the Interior
↓
Secretary of Agriculture
↓
Secretary of Commerce

HOW A BILL BECOMES A LAW

- **Senators or Representatives introduce a bill.**
  A proposed law is called a bill. The person who introduces a bill is its sponsor. A bill that requires levying taxes or spending money must begin in the House of Representatives.

- **House and Senate committees discuss the bill.**
  A bill is sent to the appropriate committee to be considered. People can speak for or against the bill at hearings.

- **Committees can change the bill.**
  Once a bill has been considered, the committee members can make any changes that they think are necessary.

- **The bill is debated in the House and Senate.**
  A majority of the House and Senate must agree on a bill to ensure its passage.

- **The bill is sent to Conference Committee.**
  The committee resolves any disagreements between the House and Senate versions of the bill.

- **Final vote in the House and Senate.**
  For a bill to become law, it must be approved by a majority of members of the House and the Senate and signed by the president.

- **The president signs the bill into law.**
  The president's signature is required for a bill to become a law. The president does not sign every bill that the full Congress approves.

- **Presidential veto.**
  The president's refusal to sign a bill is called a veto. A vetoed bill can still become law if at least two-thirds of Congress votes for it. This is called overriding the president's veto.

What are the first ten amendments called and what do they do? Write your answer on the flap.

Senate committees are made up of members of both parties. Most legislators serve on several committees. The Senate has sixteen standing committees and the House has nineteen. Standing committees are permanent. Select committees are temporary. The most powerful standing committees are the Appropriations, Armed Services, Foreign Relations, and Judiciary committees.

FOUR TYPES OF COMMITTEES

Committee	Purpose
Standing (the most important committee)	deals with bills concerning legislative matters
Select (also called Special)	handles investigations or other special matters
Conference	resolves differences in bills
Joint	deals with research and matters affecting both houses of Congress

WAR OF 1812
MONROE DOCTRINE

How can a vetoed bill become law? Write your answer on the flap.

During Britain's bombardment of Baltimore, Maryland, American poet Francis Scott Key wrote the lyrics for "The Star Spangled Banner," which later became the national anthem.

WAR OF 1812

The **War of 1812** is sometimes called "the Second War of Independence." It was fought between the United States and Great Britain from 1812 to 1815. These were the main causes of the war:

- The British set up blockades of European ports.
- The British attack and seize American merchant ships attempting to trade with France.
- The British force American sailors to serve on British ships. This is known as **impressment**.

Although there was no clear winner, the **Treaty of Ghent** was signed on December 24, 1814, and ended the war, but the treaty was not ratified by the United States until 1815. Fifteen days after the treaty was signed, the United States defeated Great Britain at the Battle of New Orleans. The major events of the war include:

- America declares war against Britain on June 18, 1812.
- Admiral Oliver Hazard Perry defeats the British fleet at the Battle of Lake Erie in 1813.
- The British burn the White House, the Capitol, and other public buildings in 1814.

MONROE DOCTRINE

In 1823, **President James Monroe** warned European nations not to interfere with any countries in North and South America. In return, Monroe promised the United States wouldn't interfere in conflicts in other parts of the world. This principle was known as the **Monroe Doctrine**. Without threats from foreign nations, Americans focused on exploring and building their new country.

In the 1840s, many Americans believed it was God's will, as well as their right, that they expand and control all of the country from the Atlantic Ocean to the Pacific. This view was also used to justify taking land away from Native Americans and Mexicans. The term for this belief, **manifest destiny**, meant that something was destined, or fated, to happen.

CHAPTER 4

Westward Expansion

In 1769, **Daniel Boone** and some friends set off from North Carolina to explore America's western regions. After crossing through an opening in the Appalachian Mountains called the **Cumberland Gap**, they found Kentucky. Boone was amazed by the rich land and plentiful game. In 1775, he led a group of settlers to Kentucky. They cut a trail to the Kentucky River and built the settlement of Boonesborough. The path Boone cut was later used by thousands of settlers on their way west. They called it the **Wilderness Road**.

OVERLAND ROUTES

Two of the major overland routes west of the Mississippi River from the early to mid 1800s were the **Oregon Trail** and the **Santa Fe Trail**. The Oregon Trail opened a path to the Northwest, while the Santa Fe Trail blazed a road to the Southwest.

PIONEERS AND FRONTIERS

1769	Daniel Boone crosses the Cumberland Gap to explore Kentucky
1787	Northwest Ordinance
1803	The Louisiana Purchase
1804	Lewis and Clark expedition
1836	The Alamo
1840s	Manifest destiny
1846–1848	Mexican War
1848	Gold rush
1862	Homestead Act

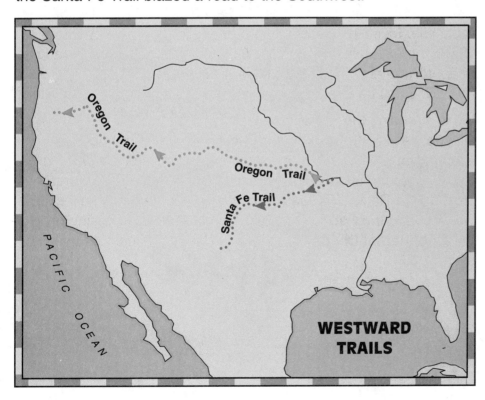

WESTWARD TRAILS

THE NORTHWEST TERRITORY
THE LOUISIANA PURCHASE
LEWIS AND CLARK EXPEDITION

THE NORTHWEST TERRITORY

In 1787, Congress passed a law called the Northwest Ordinance for governing the Northwest Territory and admitting new states to the Union. According to this law, the territory would be divided and slavery would not be allowed there. When an area had a population of sixty thousand, it could ask Congress to be admitted as a state. Ohio, Indiana, Illinois, Michigan, and Wisconsin were formed from the Northwest Territory.

THE LOUISIANA PURCHASE

What was the name of the path cut by Daniel Boone and used by settlers on their way west? Write your answer on the flap.

In 1800, Napoleon Bonaparte—who would become emperor of France—acquired Louisiana from Spain. Over time, however, American farmers increasingly shipped their goods through the port of New Orleans, and President Jefferson wanted to be sure they could continue to do so. He hoped James Madison, his Secretary of State, would be able to negotiate American rights to the port. France agreed to sell all of Louisiana rather than risk a war with the U.S. and its British ally. In 1803, Madison paid $15 million for the territory called the Louisiana Purchase, which stretched all the way from the Mississippi River to the Rocky Mountains.

LEWIS AND CLARK EXPEDITION

Lewis and Clark explored the present-day states of Idaho, Iowa, Missouri, Montana, North Dakota, Oregon, South Dakota, and Washington.

Thomas Jefferson appointed his private secretary, Meriwether Lewis, to explore and map the land acquired in the Louisiana Purchase. Including Lewis's friend and fellow Virginian William Clark, the expedition (called the Corps of Discovery) was made up of approximately fifty men. In May of 1804, the group headed out from St. Louis on the Missouri River toward the uncharted territory.

Which states were formed from the Northwest Territory? Write your answer on the flap.

While spending the winter with the Mandan Indians in North Dakota, Lewis and Clark met a Shoshone woman named Sacajawea. She became their guide and translator and was very important to the success of the expedition. When the explorers crossed the Rocky Mountains, they saw that the rivers flowed west, toward the Pacific Ocean. This marked their crossing of the Continental Divide, a mountain ridge that separates river systems.

By November 7, 1805, the expedition had reached the Pacific. They built Ft. Clatsop and spent the winter there (near present-day Astoria, Oregon). On the return voyage from Ft. Clatsop to St. Louis, Lewis and Clark divided the explorers into two groups. Lewis headed into what is present-day Montana to explore the fur-rich north. Clark headed for the Yellowstone River. At the end of the summer of 1806 they regrouped and continued east. They returned to St. Louis, Missouri, on September 23, 1806, with pages of detailed notes and drawings of the geography, wildlife, and people they had met.

LEWIS AND CLARK EXPEDITION

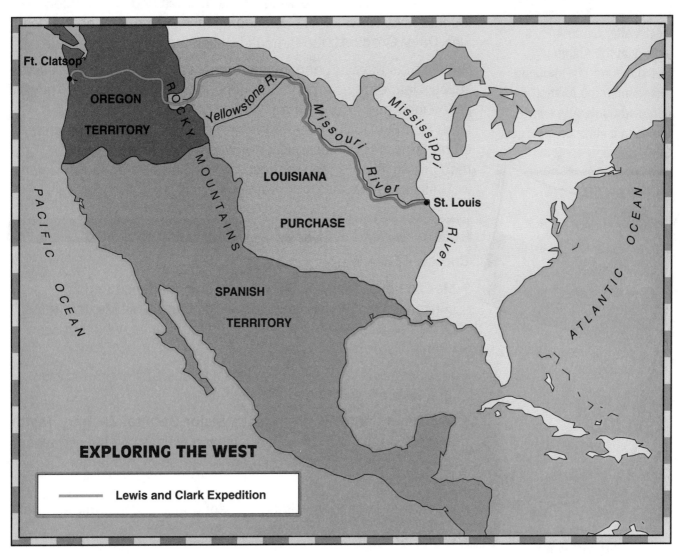

EXPLORING THE WEST

Lewis and Clark Expedition

On April 21, 1836, just six weeks after Santa Anna's victory at the Alamo, Houston's troops, shouting "Remember the Alamo!" defeated Santa Anna and his forces in a surprise attack at San Jacinto.

Flag of Texas

What do you call a mountain ridge that separates river systems? Write your answer on the flap.

THE ALAMO AND MEXICAN RULE

In the early 1800s, Texas was part of Mexico. When settlers from the United States arrived in Texas, they became Mexican citizens. Eventually, Texans resented how they were governed. This led to battles with the Mexicans. The Mexican military dictator, **General Antonio Lopez de Santa Anna**, was determined to put down the Texan rebellion. On February 23, 1836, he led five thousand soldiers in an attack on the Texas revolutionaries at the **Alamo**, an old Spanish mission-fortress in San Antonio. On March 6, 1836, Santa Anna's troops scaled the walls of the fortress and, in a fiercely fought battle, killed all 183 defenders of the Alamo. Among the dead was **Davy Crockett**, the famous frontiersman from Tennessee.

But even as Mexican and Texan forces were fighting at the Alamo, Texas's leaders declared their independence from Mexico. They called their new country the Republic of Texas (nicknamed the Lone Star Republic), and **Sam Houston** was named commander of the army. The Mexican dictator was forced to sign a treaty recognizing Texan independence. Texas's admission to the Union in 1845 led to the **Mexican War**.

MEXICAN WAR (1846–1848)

Causes of the War:

- Mexico never really accepts Texan independence and is concerned that Americans in California and New Mexico (then owned by Mexico) will also seek independence, which they eventually do.

- Americans believe Mexico's refusal to sell California and New Mexico is an obstacle to manifest destiny.

- **President James K. Polk** sends **Major General Zachary Taylor** and his small group of soldiers to land claimed by Mexico along the Rio Grande. Taylor's men are defeated by the larger Mexican army.

- Congress gives Polk authority to announce a declaration of war.

Results of the War:

- By 1847, the United States controls all of New Mexico and California.

- On February 2, 1848, Mexico signs the **Treaty of Guadalupe Hidalgo**.

- Mexico gives up all claims to Texas.

- The United States pays Mexico $15 million for New Mexico and California and agrees to respect the rights of Spanish-speaking people living there.

THE GOLD RUSH AND WESTWARD EXPANSION

The gold rush began with the discovery of gold in northern California on January 24, 1848, at **Sutter's Mill**. The crowds of people who set out to mine the gold fields in 1849 were referred to as **forty-niners**. Their push westward spurred development of the country's transportation and communication systems.

One of the early routes to the west was opened by **William Becknell**—a merchant and explorer. In 1821, he led a group of traders from St. Louis, Missouri, to Sante Fe, New Mexico. This route was known as the **Santa Fe Trail**. (See the map on page 25.)

Pioneer families traveled westward in **wagon trains**, which were made up of groups of settlers traveling in wagons and on horseback. Traveling in groups offered them greater protection from robbers or unfriendly Native Americans. The first big wagon train bound for Oregon country began in Independence, Missouri. To reach Oregon before winter, wagon trains had to leave Independence in May. The journey was 2,000 miles (3,220 km) long and took about five months. Most of the pioneers walked the entire way.

A **prairie schooner** was a wagon with a large white canvas covering similar to the sail on a schooner ship. The wagon was drawn by two or four horses or oxen. The heavier **Conestoga** wagons were pulled by a team of four to six horses.

The **Pony Express** (founded in 1860) was, for a short time, the fastest system in the country for carrying the mail. Riders mounted fresh horses waiting at stations that were spaced about 10–25 miles (16–40 km) apart. At 75 miles (121 km), the mailbag was passed to a new rider. Riders could carry the mail from St. Joseph, Missouri, to Sacramento, California, in ten days—a journey of 2,000 miles (3,220 km) that normally took two to three weeks by stagecoach. Though the route was dangerous, only one mail delivery was ever lost. The Pony Express went bankrupt when the Pacific Telegraph Company completed the installation of telegraph wires to San Francisco in 1861, enabling messages to be sent in seconds.

TRAILS, RAILS, AND WAGONS

1821	Santa Fe Trail/William Becknell
1828	B&O Railroad
1840s	Wagon trains
1860	Pony Express founded
1869	Completion of transcontinental railroad

Conestoga Wagon

RAIL TRAVEL

Railroads were being built through territories that were not yet states. Construction on the Baltimore and Ohio (B&O) Railroad was begun in 1828 by some merchants in Baltimore, Maryland. At first, horses and sails pulled the cars along wooden tracks that were covered with strips of iron. In 1830, a steam-powered locomotive called *Tom Thumb* replaced the horses and sails.

Who were the forty-niners? Write your answer on the flap.

To connect the eastern and western sections of the first **transcontinental railroad**, the **Union Pacific Railroad** began laying tracks from Omaha, Nebraska, westward. Rails from the **Central Pacific Railroad** were laid from Sacramento, California, eastward. Tracks from both railroads met on May 10, 1869, in **Promontory, Utah**.

Compared with stagecoach or horseback, rail travel offered many advantages. For example:

- Travel time was reduced. (In 1800, it took six weeks to travel from New York to Chicago. By 1860, it took two days.)
- Materials and goods could be shipped more cheaply and faster.
- Distant towns could be reached more easily, expanding the market for goods.
- News traveled faster, uniting people.

CRIMES OF EXPANSION

Resettlement:

Native Americans had treaties, or agreements, with the United States government that protected their land. But **President Andrew Jackson** didn't recognize their rights. When U.S. citizens wanted the lands of the Southeast belonging to the Cherokee, Creek, Chickasaw, Choctaw, and Seminole nations, Jackson encouraged Congress in 1830 to pass the **Indian Removal Act**. This act forced Native Americans to resettle, or move, onto reservations in the west.

Where did the tracks for the first transcontinental railroad meet? Write your answer on the flap.

Trail of Tears:

In the winter of 1838, more than thirteen thousand Cherokees were removed from their homes by the United States Army. They were forced to march to Oklahoma, 800 miles (1,288 km) away. With little food or shelter, four thousand Native Americans died along the way. The long, sad journey is known as the **Trail of Tears**. By 1900, all Native Americans had been forced onto reservations.

Wounded Knee:

In the late 1880s, the Sioux began performing a ritual called the ghost dance. They believed this would result in the return of their lands, the disappearance of the whites, and a life of eternal peace. Nearby white settlers, frightened by the ritual, wanted it stopped. On September 29, 1890, the unarmed Sioux were placed in a camp near Wounded Knee Creek in South Dakota. The U.S. Cavalry killed over two hundred Sioux men, women, and children.

The Wounded Knee massacre was one of many crimes the United States people committed against Native Americans.

CHAPTER 5

A Nation Weighs Slavery

As Americans continued to move west, the question of whether or not slavery would be allowed to spread into the new territories became an important issue. In 1818, when the Territory of Missouri (which was part of the Louisiana Purchase) applied for admission to the Union as a slave state, it set off a bitter debate in Congress.

MISSOURI COMPROMISE (1820)

The **Missouri Compromise** was a plan to keep the number of free and slave states the same so that they would continue to be equally represented in the Senate. To do so, Congress permitted Missouri to enter the Union as a slave state and Maine as a free state. Slavery was banned in all other territories of the Louisiana Purchase north of Missouri's southern border.

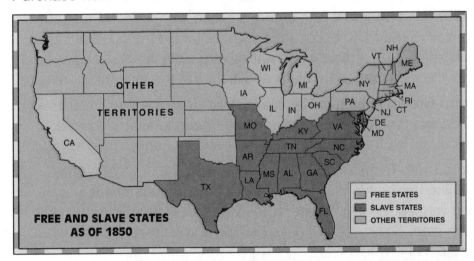

FREE AND SLAVE STATES AS OF 1850

FREE STATES
SLAVE STATES
OTHER TERRITORIES

COMPROMISE OF 1850

To lessen the growing tension between pro-slavery Southern states and antislavery Northern states, Congress adopted several measures that became known as the **Compromise of 1850**. The main points of the Compromise are outlined in the sidebar on the right.

The Compromise of 1850 stated that:

• California would enter the Union as a free state.

• The Mexican Cession would be divided into the territories of New Mexico and Utah. Voters in these territories would decide the slavery issue for themselves.

• There would be no slave trade in Washington, D.C., but Congress had no authority to ban the trade between slave states.

• A fugitive-slave law required Northern citizens to return runaway slaves to their Southern owners. Letting a slave escape meant a $1,000 fine and jail time. (Many Northerners opposed or totally ignored this law.)

DRED SCOTT DECISION

Dred Scott was a slave in Missouri. He sued for his freedom on the grounds that he had lived for several years with his owner in free states. In 1857, the Supreme Court rejected Scott's argument. The Court ruled that a black man "had no rights which white men were bound to respect" and that blacks were not citizens of the United States.

LINCOLN-DOUGLAS DEBATES

Stephen Douglas and **Abraham Lincoln** were opponents in the 1858 election to the U.S. Senate from Illinois. Slavery was the main issue in seven public debates between them. Douglas, a Democrat, was pro-slavery. Lincoln, a Republican, believed the United States would not survive if it were "half slave and half free." Though Douglas won the Senate election, two years later Lincoln was elected the sixteenth president of the United States.

Frederick Douglass

ABOLITIONISTS

People who believed slavery should be abolished were called **abolitionists**. An outspoken white abolitionist named **William Lloyd Garrison** began publishing an antislavery newspaper, *The Liberator*, in Massachusetts in 1831.

Frederick Douglass was born a slave in Maryland. He taught himself to read and escaped to Boston. In 1847, Douglass began publishing the *North Star*, an antislavery newspaper. Douglass was the most important black abolitionist of the nineteenth century.

John Brown moved to Kansas to help make it a free state. He killed five pro-slavery settlers. He was hanged after leading a failed raid on the federal arsenal at Harpers Ferry, Virginia.

Sojourner Truth was born a slave in New York in 1797. After gaining her freedom in 1828, she fought for the rights of blacks and women. When opponents insisted that women were weaker than men, she replied: "I have plowed and planted and gathered. And ain't I a woman?"

Harriet Tubman

The most famous conductor on the "railroad" was Harriet Tubman, an escaped slave, who helped more than three hundred people find safety.

THE UNDERGROUND RAILROAD

A series of secret escape routes and hiding places (such as homes and farms) was known as the **Underground Railroad**, where runaway slaves could find food and shelter while fleeing to freedom in the Northern states and in Canada. Guides to safety were known as "conductors," and hiding places were "stations."

CHAPTER 6

American Civil War

In a **civil war**, people of the same country fight against each other. The American Civil War (1861–1865) began with the goal of restoring harmony to the Union. It later became a war to end slavery. During the four years of the war, at least 622,000 people were killed in battle—364,000 in the North and 258,000 in the South. At least that many more were wounded, and many others died of disease and sickness. Most of the battles were fought in the South, leaving the land and economy in ruins. Northern, or **Union**, soldiers wore blue uniforms and were called blues or Billy Yanks. **Confederates**, or soldiers for the South, wore gray and were called grays, rebels, or Johnny Rebs.

Causes of the War:

- Northerners oppose the **Fugitive Slave Law of 1850** requiring all citizens to aid in the capture of runaway slaves.

- In 1860, Abraham Lincoln is nominated for president. He opposes slavery and **secession**—the right of states to secede or leave the Union. Southerners believe they will lose power in the national government.

- Southern Democrats support slavery in the territories, but Northern Democrats are opposed. This issue divides the North and South, and the party splits.

- Southern Democrats believe that with an opponent of slavery in the White House (Lincoln), they must secede from the Union.

- South Carolina secedes and is soon followed by five other states that have large populations of slaves and abundant cotton.

- The six states form the **Confederate States of America**, write a constitution, and elect **Jefferson Davis** of Mississippi as their president. Eventually, eleven states form the Confederacy.

- On April 12, 1861, Confederates fire on **Fort Sumter** in South Carolina. This begins the American Civil War.

Union and Confederate Flags

Results of the War:

- At least 622,000 Americans are killed.
- The South's economy is destroyed, but the Union is preserved.
- Four million blacks gain their freedom.
- The authority of the federal government is expanded.
- The Northern economy booms.

BALANCE OF POWER: THE AMERICAN CIVIL WAR

	Advantages	Disadvantages
South	• fighting in familiar territory with a passion to defend their property and way of life • skilled hunters, horsemen, riflemen • outstanding military leaders	• fewer people than the North • fewer factories to make war supplies such as guns, cannon, and ammunition • fewer railroads for moving troops and supplies • blockaded ports prevent South from selling cotton and buying supplies
North	• larger population • more factories • more railroads, roads, and canals to move troops and supplies • strong navy	• had to fight in unfamiliar territory • fewer skilled military leaders

What marked the beginning of the Civil War? Write your answer on the flap.

Which was the first state to secede from the Union? Write your answer on the flap.

SIDES DRAWN IN THE CIVIL WAR

Confederate (Slave states)	Union (Free states)	Union (Slave states, also known as border states)
Alabama	California	Delaware
Arkansas	Connecticut	Kentucky
Florida	Illinois	Maryland
Georgia	Indiana	Missouri
Louisiana	Iowa	West Virginia*
Mississippi	Kansas	
North Carolina	Maine	*When Virginia seceded, people in the western part of the state formed their own government and joined the Union in 1863 as a separate state.
South Carolina	Massachusetts	
Tennessee	Michigan	
Texas	Minnesota	
Virginia	New Hampshire	
	New Jersey	
	New York	
	Ohio	
	Oregon	
	Pennsylvania	
	Rhode Island	
	Vermont	
	Wisconsin	

Who was the president of the Confederate States of America? Write your answer on the flap.

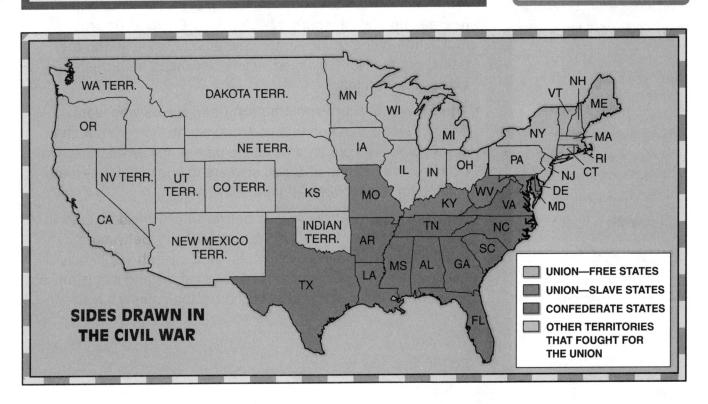

SIDES DRAWN IN THE CIVIL WAR

UNION—FREE STATES
UNION—SLAVE STATES
CONFEDERATE STATES
OTHER TERRITORIES THAT FOUGHT FOR THE UNION

MAJOR EVENTS OF THE WAR

MAJOR EVENTS OF THE WAR

- The **Battle of Bull Run** (also called the **Battle of Manassas**) was the first fight between the Union and Confederate armies and ended in a Confederate victory.

- President Lincoln offered **Robert E. Lee** of Virginia field command of the Union forces, but Lee refused it. Though he was opposed to slavery and secession, he could not fight against his fellow Southerners. Lee resigned from the U.S. Army and became commander of the Confederate forces. Both Northerners and Southerners considered Lee the country's most brilliant military leader.

- The *Merrimack* was an abandoned Union warship that the Confederates covered with thick iron plates. In battle, cannon-balls bounced off it. The Union built its own **ironclad**, the *Monitor*. When the *Merrimack* and the *Monitor* met, neither could damage the other, and both retreated.

- On April 6, 1862, **General Ulysses S. Grant** defeated the Confederates at the small village of Shiloh in Tennessee. More Americans died in one day at the **Battle of Shiloh** (nearly 24,000) than in the American Revolution, the War of 1812, and the Mexican War combined. Such huge losses were typical of many Civil War battles.

- Attempting to invade the North, Lee was met at **Antietam** (a creek near Sharpsburg, Maryland) by **General George McClellan** of the Union Army. Neither side actually won the battle, but the North claimed victory because Lee retreated across the Potomac.

- The **Emancipation Proclamation** freed slaves who were living in states that had rebelled against the Union. Though no slaves actually were set free at the time of the proclamation, it bolstered the morale of Union soldiers to know that they were fighting for a just cause—to end slavery.

- The **Gettysburg Address** was delivered by President Lincoln at the dedication of the Civil War cemetery in Gettysburg, Pennsylvania. Lincoln believed his short speech was a failure, but its sincere expression of American values and ideals makes it one of the most admired speeches in the country's history.

- General Grant, now promoted to commander-in-chief of the Union army, ordered generals **Philip Henry Sheridan** and **William Tecumseh Sherman** to destroy everything in the South that might be of any use to the enemy. On Sherman's march from **Atlanta** to the Atlantic Ocean, he burned everything in his path. This strategy, called **total war**, caused much suffering for civilians.

- On April 9, 1865, General Robert E. Lee surrendered to General Ulysses S. Grant in a small Virginia town named **Appomattox Court House**. Grant allowed the defeated Confederate soldiers to keep their horses and mules but not their rifles. Officers were allowed to keep their pistols.

- Less than a week after the war ended, Lincoln was assassinated while watching a play at Ford's Theater in Washington, D.C. The assassin, an actor named **John Wilkes Booth**, shot Lincoln in the back of the head. The President died the next morning. Booth escaped but was caught and killed twelve days later.

Abraham Lincoln

RECONSTRUCTION (1865–1877)

After the Civil War, there was a twelve-year period called **Reconstruction**, during which the South was rebuilt. Lincoln wanted the South to rejoin the Union quickly so Reconstruction and reuniting the country could begin as soon as possible. But a group in Congress, known as **Radical Republicans**, was angry that the South had not accepted the end of slavery. During the period from 1866 to 1877, known as Radical Reconstruction, legislation initiated by the Radical Republicans aimed to weaken anti-black sentiment in the South.

The **Freedmen's Bureau** was a federal program begun in 1865 to provide food, clothing, legal aid, and medical care to former slaves and poor whites in the South. It also laid the foundation for the South's public school system and established four universities.

Many people in the South, mostly plantation owners, still resented Northerners. They called Southern whites who cooperated with the Republican government **scalawags** and considered them to be traitors. In fact, most so-called scalawags were nonslaveholding small farmers who had been loyal to the Union during the Civil War. Northerners who arrived during Reconstruction were called **carpetbaggers**, meaning they had quickly tossed their belongings in a carpetbag suitcase and hurried to the South in hopes of getting rich quick. But many carpetbaggers had good intentions. They included teachers, Freedmen's Bureau agents, former Union soldiers, missionaries, and honest businessmen.

What two ironclad ships battled each other? Write your answer on the flap.

RECONSTRUCTION

POSTWAR REGRESSION

BIRTH OF THE CIVIL RIGHTS MOVEMENT

What was the term for rebuilding the South after the Civil War? Write your answer on the flap.

The economic and social scars of Reconstruction remained. Many Southerners moved to the North because there were few job opportunities in the South. Although blacks were no longer slaves, they were not fully accepted in society. Literacy tests and poll tests kept some blacks from voting in elections.

Which amendment granted citizenship to all former slaves? Write your answer on the flap.

Legislation Passed During Reconstruction:

- The Thirteenth Amendment freed all slaves (1865).
- The Civil Rights Act granted citizenship to all persons born in the United States (1866). Republicans in Congress overrode President Andrew Johnson's veto to pass this bill.
- The Fourteenth Amendment granted citizenship to all former slaves and guaranteed all citizens "equal protection under the law" (1868). Courts were asked to enforce this amendment.
- The Fifteenth Amendment gave African-American men the right to vote (1870).
- The Compromise of 1877 ended Reconstruction.

POSTWAR REGRESSION

Many legislatures in the South passed **Black Codes**—laws that limited the rights and economic opportunities of blacks. With so many restrictions on what they could do, most blacks had to continue working as plantation laborers. With the Civil Rights Act of 1866, the Radical Republicans tried to correct this injustice.

Jim Crow laws were passed in Southern states, making it legal to keep blacks and whites **segregated**, or separate from each other. The laws applied almost everywhere—in schools, restaurants, theaters, hospitals, buses, trains, playgrounds, and cemeteries.

The **Ku Klux Klan (KKK)** was a secret terrorist society formed by white Southerners to keep blacks from voting or enjoying other rights of citizenship. Dressed in robes and hoods to hide their identities, Klansmen threatened, beat, and murdered blacks and their white supporters throughout the South. Sometimes the Klansmen burned crosses on people's property to frighten them.

BIRTH OF THE CIVIL RIGHTS MOVEMENT

Booker T. Washington was born a slave. After the Civil War, he attended a trade school established by the Freedmen's Bureau and became a teacher. Washington stressed to his students the importance of learning a skill so they would be able to earn a living. He angered some civil rights leaders by urging blacks to concentrate on economic self-reliance rather than on achieving social equality.

W.E.B. DuBois, a strong supporter of racial equality, was the first black awarded a doctoral degree from Harvard. In 1909, DuBois helped create the **National Association for the Advancement of Colored People (NAACP)**. The goal of the NAACP was to eliminate discrimination against blacks. The organization still exists today.

CHAPTER 7

Industrial Revolution

CHANGES—GOOD AND BAD

In the early nineteenth century, most Americans lived on small farms and produced almost everything they needed. In the period before the Civil War, however, instead of goods being made at home or in workshops with simple tools, they were mass-produced with machines in factories. The term **Industrial Revolution** was first used to describe this new means of production, and the enormous changes that resulted in the way people lived and worked.

The First Industrial Revolution in the United States began before the Civil War. The Second Industrial Revolution took place after the war.

CHANGES—GOOD AND BAD

On the farm, the effects of the Industrial Revolution seemed generally positive. For example, tractors gradually replaced plow horses, and new farm equipment and fertilizers increased crop production. Not all farmers could afford the equipment or supplies, and eventually fewer farmers were needed since machines could do much of their work. As a result, many farmers were forced to leave their farms and their homes. In the cities, however, for each good result of the Industrial Revolution there was a negative one. Some of these problems are listed in the table below.

INDUSTRIAL REVOLUTION: PRO AND CON

Advantages	Disadvantages
• spread of factory system created new jobs	• women and children in factories worked twelve-hour days, six days a week; women and children were paid less than men; machines were dangerous
• growth of cities	• increase of crime, pollution, disease in cities
• assembly lines increased production	• work was boring, exhausting
• standard of living improved for many	• the few people who became enormously rich did so at the expense of the many

CAPITALISTS, ROBBER BARONS, AND MONOPOLIES

AMERICAN INVENTORS/INVENTIONS

Year	Inventor	Invention
1790	Samuel Slater and Moses Brown	spinning mill
1793	Eli Whitney	cotton gin
1807	Robert Fulton	steamboat
1837	Samuel Morse	telegraph
1846	Elias Howe	sewing machine
1872	Elijah McCoy	device that oiled moving parts of machines
1876	Alexander Graham Bell	telephone
1878	Anna Baldwin	milking machine
1879	Thomas Alva Edison	electric lightbulb
1888	George Eastman	portable camera
1903	Wilbur and Orville Wright	propeller airplane
1908	Henry Ford	Model T car

It took Thomas Edison 6,000 tries to develop the lightbulb. He patented 1,093 inventions in his lifetime.

SOME ROBBER BARONS AND THEIR MONOPOLIES

Cornelius Vanderbilt—railroads

Andrew Carnegie—steel

John D. Rockefeller—oil

CAPITALISTS, ROBBER BARONS, AND MONOPOLIES

People with enough money to own machines and factories during the Industrial Revolution were called **capitalists** ("capital" means money or resources). Some capitalists of the late nineteenth century were called **robber barons**. These men became enormously rich by building and controlling huge industries, but they also drove smaller companies out of business and didn't always treat their workers fairly.

Complete control over an industry by one person or company is known as a **monopoly**. Monopolies prevent competition between businesses, which means consumers cannot shop around to find better prices for goods. Monopolies of major industries by robber barons eventually led to government regulations. The first legislation passed to limit monopolies was the **Sherman Antitrust Act** in 1890, which made it illegal for any person or company to limit trade through a monopoly.

LABOR UNIONS

Before the development of **labor unions**, laborers had almost no say about their wages or working conditions. And because there was so much competition for jobs, anyone who complained was usually fired and quickly replaced by another worker. As members of a union, workers present a united front when it comes to making demands to management and, therefore, have a much better bargaining position. One of the first national labor unions, **Knights of Labor**, was founded by **Uriah Stephens** in 1869. All workers were welcome to join regardless of their race, creed, or craft.

In 1886, Samuel Gompers co-founded and became the first president of the **American Federation of Labor (AFL)**. Its bias toward skilled workers deeply divided members along racial, gender, and ethnic lines. Gompers urged his members to vote for political candidates who would support the goals of the union.

John L. Lewis, founder of the **Committee for Industrial Organization (CIO)**, organized all workers in a single industry into one union. He led several strikes against the automobile, steel, and coal industries that resulted in improved conditions for workers. In 1955, the AFL and CIO merged. The AFL-CIO's first president was **George Meany**.

COMMON LABOR TERMS

- **Collective bargaining**: negotiations between employers and labor union representatives about terms and conditions of employment. If an industry vital to national security is affected, government officials may also be involved in the negotiations.

- **Picketing**: striking workers gather near their place of employment to **picket**, or protest with signs and slogans, thereby making the public aware of disagreements and gathering support for the union position. Violence by or against pickets is illegal.

- **Strike**: an organized work stoppage to pressure employers into improving work conditions or pay rates, or to protest unfair labor practices. In 1842, Massachusetts courts were the first to declare workers had the right to strike. Until then, strikes were illegal and strikers could be arrested.

- **Sympathy strike**: one union stops work to show support for another union already on strike.

What is complete control over an industry called? Write your answer on the flap.

UNION GOALS
- eight-hour workday
- abolition of convict labor
- no child labor under age fourteen
- equal opportunities and wages for women

IMMIGRATION
SPANISH-AMERICAN WAR

IMMIGRATION

People who come to live in a new country are **immigrants**. Millions of immigrants journeyed to the United States in the late 1800s and early 1900s. Many arrived at **Ellis Island**, a processing center near the Statue of Liberty in New York harbor. Immigrants built railroads and bridges, worked in mines and factories, and supplied much of the labor that shaped the United States into a modern industrial nation.

SPANISH-AMERICAN WAR (1898)

Cubans, seeking their independence from Spain, had rebelled against that country. Many Americans were sympathetic with the Cuban cause and aided the leaders of the revolt. Under the guise of protecting Americans and their property in Cuba, the United States sent a battleship, the *Maine*, to Cuba. When it blew up in Havana harbor, Spain was blamed.

The entire war lasted only four months. The first battle took place in the Philippines (which also belonged to Spain). **Theodore Roosevelt** formed a group of volunteers, made up of cowboys and his Ivy-League college classmates, which he called the **Rough Riders**. Led by Roosevelt, the Rough Riders fought their way up Kettle Hill to take the city of Santiago, Cuba, on July 1, 1898. Two weeks later, Spain surrendered. The United States had won the war.

Causes of the War:

- Spain refuses to grant Cuba independence.
- Aboard the *Maine,* 266 Americans are killed when it mysteriously explodes in the harbor of Havana on February 15, 1898.
- The United States blockades Cuban ports, leading to war between Spain and the United States.

Results of the War:

- Cuba becomes an independent nation.
- The United States acquires the Philippines (until 1946), Guam, and Puerto Rico.
- Theodore Roosevelt becomes nationally known and a popular hero. In 1901 he becomes the twenty-sixth president of the United States.
- The United States becomes an influential world power.

YELLOW JOURNALISM
Newspaper reporting that relies on sensational pictures, shocking headlines, and one-sided views in order to influence public opinion or arouse emotional responses is referred to as yellow journalism. This type of reporting was used to increase newspaper circulation and was widespread during the coverage of the Spanish-American War by a sensationalistic press that was pro-Cuba and anti-Spain.

What was the AFL and who co-founded it? Write your answer on the flap.

What is an organized work stoppage called? Write your answer on the flap.

CHAPTER 8

The Early Twentieth Century

WORLD WAR I (1914–1918)

On June 28, 1914, **Archduke Francis Ferdinand**, heir to the Austrian and Hungarian thrones, was assassinated by a Serbian. This was the immediate cause of **World War I (1914–1918)**. Though it began as a local war between Austria-Hungary and Serbia, most of Europe became involved. Eventually thirty-two nations were in conflict, siding with either the **Allies** or the **Central Powers**. The United States joined the Allies when it declared war on Germany on April 6, 1917.

New weapons, such as machine guns, grenades, poison gas, tanks, airplanes, and submarines (called U-boats), made the fighting fierce. In fact, it was the introduction of submarine warfare by Germany that finally drew the United States into the war. When a German U-boat sank an unarmed British ship, the *Lusitania*, 1,198 people were killed, among them 128 Americans. This, along with the later sinking of American merchant ships by the Germans, forced the United States to abandon its policy of neutrality (a refusal to take sides).

Causes of the War:

- **Nationalism** (extreme allegiance to a particular ethnic group) flourishes.
- Political and economic rivalry rages among nations.
- Armies and navies continue to expand.
- Two hostile military alliances are formed: **Triple Alliance** (Germany, Austria-Hungary, and Italy) and **Triple Entente** (Great Britain, France, and Russia).

Results of the War:

- Nearly ten million soldiers are killed in battle.
- Germany's military is practically eliminated.
- Germany loses territory and is ordered to make **reparations** (financial payments to Allied countries for war-related costs).

TIME LINE	
1914	Archduke Ferdinand assassinated
1915	German U-boat sinks *Lusitania*
1917	U.S. enters WWI
1918	Armistice (an end to the fighting) declared
1919	Treaty of Versailles signed

The United States suffered 320,000 casualties. The war's total casualties were approximately 37 million, including civilian deaths and wounded.

43

What ignited World War I? Write your answer on the flap.

- The economic hardship, suffering, and humiliation the Germans experience over the terms of the Treaty of Versailles lay the foundation for World War II.

TRENCH WARFARE

The heaviest fighting of the war occurred mostly on the **western front** (along the borders of France and Germany). Soldiers lived, fought, and died by the millions in muddy ditches called trenches that they dug on the battlefield. Firing trenches were backed up by cover trenches in case the enemy overran the first line of defense. Off-duty troops lived in support trenches. Supplies, food, and fresh troops were moved to the firing trenches along reserve and communications trenches. The deadly area between the trenches of the opposing armies was called no man's land.

SIDES DRAWN IN WORLD WAR I

	Major Allies
	Central Powers
	Neutral Countries

POSTWAR TREATIES

Leaders from the United States, Great Britain, France, and Italy negotiated the **Treaty of Versailles** at the Paris Peace Conference in 1919. (The United States signed a separate peace treaty, the **Treaty of Berlin**, with Germany in August 1921.) Although Italy was part of the Triple Alliance it joined the war in 1914 on the side of the Allies. Italy did not believe it had to honor the Triple Alliance because it didn't think Austria-Hungary had begun the war in self-defense. **President Woodrow Wilson** was determined to form an organization to settle serious conflicts without war. This was the

League of Nations, the world's first peacekeeping body. But many politicians in the United States were opposed to joining the League. They believed membership would obligate the country to become involved in future European conflicts.

WOMEN'S RIGHT TO VOTE

Elizabeth Cady Stanton and Lucretia Coffin Mott worked as antislavery reformers. They also were determined to secure equal rights for women. In 1848, at a convention in Seneca Falls, New York, Cady Stanton read a declaration demanding equal rights for women at work, school, and church. The boldest demand for women, though, was for suffrage—the right to vote. Susan B. Anthony, another loyal reformer, devoted fifty years of her life to traveling around the country and speaking about women's rights. By 1900, women in a few states had been granted suffrage. All women in the United States finally achieved the right to vote when the Nineteenth Amendment was passed in 1920.

GOOD TIMES AND THE GREAT DEPRESSION

The period from 1920 to 1929 is often called the Roaring Twenties. It was known for good times and great changes. The war was over, and industries were growing. Radio and movies provided news and entertainment, cars made travel easier, and people were eager to spend money. Most workers were confident about the future. They were earning good wages and wanted to enjoy themselves.

But taxes were rising. Many people spent more than they earned and invested their money in the stock market, buying shares in publicly traded companies on credit. Then, in October of 1929, the stock market crashed. Most stocks became worthless, and many people lost all of their money. Because people had less money to spend, factories stopped producing goods and laid off workers. By 1932, one out of every four workers in the country was unemployed.

Name four of the major countries that made up the Allied powers. Write your answer on the flap.

Suffragette

THE GREAT DEPRESSION

In economics, **a depression** is a period of low production and sales, and high rates of business failures and unemployment. The **Great Depression**, beginning after the crash of the stock market and lasting for ten years, was the worst economic decline in the history of the United States. Businesses went bankrupt and banks collapsed. Hundreds of thousands of Americans—hungry, jobless, and homeless—waited in line for free food offered by charities.

What organization was formed after WWI in hopes of preventing future wars? Write your answer on the flap.

Farmers also suffered during the Great Depression. They weren't able to sell their crops and, having no income, couldn't pay back money they had borrowed to buy land and supplies. Banks took over the farms. On the Great Plains there was a terrible drought. Strong winds blew the loose, dry soil into huge black clouds of dust. The dust storms in Texas, Oklahoma, Kansas, Nebraska, and Colorado were so frequent and severe, the region was known as the **Dust Bowl**. Thousands of farmers were unable to grow crops in the ruined land. They were forced to leave their homes in search of work elsewhere.

President Herbert Hoover had no program for ending the Depression—and he didn't really believe it was the federal government's responsibility to do so. In 1932, Hoover, a Republican, lost the presidential election to **Franklin Delano Roosevelt**, a Democrat.

Herbert Hoover

FRANKLIN DELANO ROOSEVELT

The thirty-second president of the United States was **Franklin Delano Roosevelt**. FDR was in office for more than twelve years, longer than any other president, and he died in office. In February 1951, the Twenty-second Amendment was passed stating that "no person shall be elected to the office of president more than twice...." Eight years became the limit.

FDR'S NEW DEAL (1933–1939)

President Roosevelt believed it was the "duty of the federal government to keep its citizens from starving." He promised the American people a "new deal." Along with a group of advisers known as the Brain Trust, FDR developed programs for his **New Deal**. The goal of the programs was to combat the economic crisis and put people back to work.

New Deal Programs, Acts, and Agencies:

- **Glass-Steagall Act**—created a system for enforcing stricter banking rules that restored confidence in banking

- **Federal Deposit Insurance Corporation (FDIC)**—provided insurance for bank deposits

- **Securities and Exchange Commission (SEC)**—maintained tighter regulation of the securities (stock) market

- **Federal Housing Administration (FHA)**—offered mortgage relief for farmers and homeowners and loan guarantees for home-buyers

- **Federal Emergency Relief Administration (FERA)**—helped more than twenty million people by giving relief grants to states

- **Works Progress Administration (WPA)**—provided construction jobs for unskilled workers and projects for writers and artists

- **Civilian Conservation Corps (CCC)**—provided training and jobs for about three million young men

- **Tennessee Valley Authority (TVA)**—provided funds to build dams, resulting in low-cost electrical power throughout the Tennessee Valley

- **Agricultural Adjustment Administration (AAA)** (declared unconstitutional by the Supreme Court in 1936)—guaranteed prices for crops and offered low-cost loans to farmers

Franklin Delano Roosevelt

In terms of the economy, what is a depression? Write your answer on the flap.

- **National Recovery Administration (NRA)**—approved and enforced work codes and safety regulations for various industries

- **Public Works Administration (PWA)**—hired jobless workers to build bridges, dams, power plants, roads, parks, and airports

- **National Labor Relations Act**—guaranteed workers the right to organize and bargain through unions

- **Fair Labor Standards**—established minimum wages and maximum number of working hours; set a minimum age of sixteen for workers

- **Social Security Act**—a system of enforced savings through payroll deductions aiming to ensure retirement funds, unemployment insurance, and welfare grants

NEW DEAL SCORECARD

Even with massive government aid, at the end of the New Deal many businesses had not recovered. In 1940, nearly fifteen percent of the nation's workforce still did not have jobs. Although some people questioned whether the New Deal programs had really benefited the country, it was generally agreed that most people had at least been given hope for the future. It wasn't until 1942, when the country entered World War II, that the Great Depression finally ended. The necessity of producing vast amounts of war materials provided so many jobs that by 1944 the unemployment rate had fallen to about one percent.

The Great Depression changed the philosophy of how the government spent money. Prior to the depression, the government tried not to spend more money than it collected. But to support the New Deal programs, the government used deficit spending (meaning it spent money that it didn't really have).

CHAPTER 9

World War II and Beyond

WORLD WAR II (1939–1945): PLAYERS AND ISSUES

The terms of the peace treaties that were signed at the end of World War I left the German economy in ruins and brought great hardship and humiliation to the German people. An economic depression in Europe added to the disorder. The Germans were encouraged by Adolf Hitler—the racist leader of Germany's **National Socialist German Workers' (Nazi)** party—to believe that other nations were responsible for their country's difficulties. Hitler told his followers that "pure" Germans were a superior race.

In this unsettled atmosphere, militarism began to take hold, and Hitler quickly gained power. In 1933, he became dictator of Germany. Because the terms of the treaties ending World War I had not been adequately enforced, Hitler was able to assemble the strongest army in the world, and in 1939, he invaded Poland, leading to the start of **World War II**. Italy and Japan sided with Hitler, forming the major **Axis powers**. They fought against the **Allies**. The majority of Americans did not want the country to enter the war. After the war began, President Franklin D. Roosevelt announced that the United States would remain neutral, but he urged all aid "short of war" to the Allies. Congress soon changed U.S. laws forbidding the sale of arms to warring nations so that weapons could be sold to Britain and France. When the Allies no longer had the money to buy arms, Roosevelt proposed the Lend-Lease Act, which allowed the U.S. to lend or lease raw materials, equipment, and weapons to any nation fighting the Axis.

On December 7, 1941, "a date that will live in infamy," as President Roosevelt described it, Japanese fighters bombed **Pearl Harbor**, a U.S. naval base in Hawaii. Most of the American Pacific fleet and hundreds of aircraft were destroyed, and about twenty-five hundred Americans were killed. The day after the surprise attack, the United States entered the war on the side of the Allies.

The U.S. government developed a fictional character, Rosie the Riveter, to encourage women to support the war effort by taking jobs in factories, fields, and mines. With Rosie as a role model, more than six million women joined the workforce during the war. Although most of them lost their jobs when the men returned, working outside of the home had become more acceptable for middle-class women than it had been before the war.

Rosie the Riveter

WORLD WAR II: PLAYERS AND ISSUES

Causes of the War:

- Germany, Italy, and Japan resent the terms of the Treaty of Versailles (signed after the end of World War I). Their bitter feelings help lead to World War II.
- Germany is angry about reparations payments and loss of land.
- Italy is dissatisfied with the amount of territory it gained.
- Japan is disappointed about not getting control of China.

Results of the War:

- Germany and Japan are defeated.
- Much of Europe is devastated.
- The **Marshall Plan** (named for U.S. Secretary of State George Marshall) is created to help rebuild Europe.
- Germany is divided. East Germany becomes communist; West Germany becomes a democracy. (East and West Germany are reunited in October 1990 as a democratic country.)
- Japan forms a more democratic government.
- The Soviet Union and the United States are new world powers.
- Soviet and American rivalry leads to the Cold War.

What day was Pearl Harbor bombed, and what did President Roosevelt call it? Write your answer on the flap.

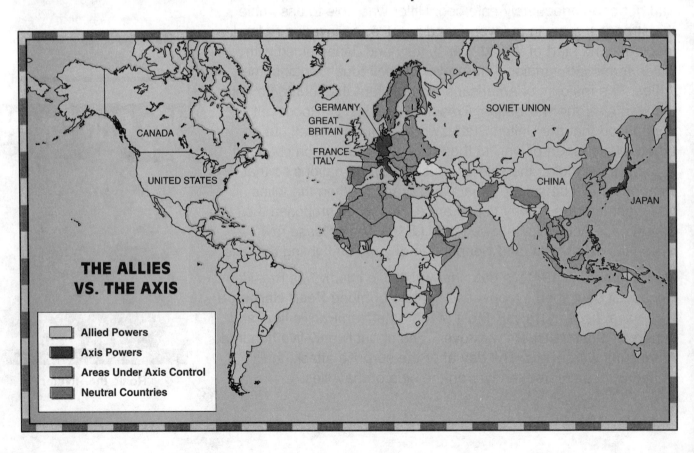

THE ALLIES VS. THE AXIS

- Allied Powers
- Axis Powers
- Areas Under Axis Control
- Neutral Countries

50

MAJOR EVENTS OF THE WAR

1939 March 15 Germany invades Czechoslovakia.
Aug. 23 Hitler and Stalin sign nonaggression pact.
Sept. 1 Germany invades Poland.
Sept. 3 Great Britain and France declare war on Germany.
Nov. 30 Soviet Union invades Finland.

1940 April 9 Germany invades Denmark and Norway.
May 10 Germany attacks Belgium, the Netherlands, Luxembourg; Winston Churchill becomes Prime Minister of Great Britain.
June 5 Germany attacks France.
June 10 Italy declares war on Great Britain and France.

1941 June 22 Germany attacks Soviet Union.
Dec. 4 Soviets launch massive counterattack, and Germany loses Moscow.
Dec. 7 Japan bombs Pearl Harbor in Hawaii.
Dec. 8 United States declares war on Japan and Germany.

1942 June 4 U.S. Navy sinks four Japanese carriers and wins Battle of Midway and control of Pacific.
Aug. 25 Germans begin five-month siege of Stalingrad.

1943 Feb. 2 Germans surrender at Stalingrad.
May 13 Axis troops surrender in North Africa.

1944 June 6 **D-Day**: Allied invasion of Normandy, France (held by the Germans), with greatest naval and air fleet ever assembled.
Aug. 25 Paris is liberated from German occupation.
Dec. 16 **Battle of the Bulge**: Germans create a "bulge" in the Allied lines.

1945 April 12 President Roosevelt dies, and Harry Truman becomes president.
April 30 Adolf Hitler commits suicide.
May 7 Germany surrenders.
May 8 **V-E Day** (Victory in Europe).
June 21 U.S. occupies Okinawa.
Aug. 6 U.S. B-29 bomber the *Enola Gay* drops atomic bomb on **Hiroshima**, a city in Japan.
Aug. 9 U.S. drops atomic bomb on **Nagasaki**, Japan.
Sept. 2 Japan surrenders.

What was the purpose of the Marshall Plan? Write your answer on the flap.

51

THE HOLOCAUST
ECONOMIC BOOM

THE HOLOCAUST

The term **holocaust** means "a terrible human disaster." When people talk about the Holocaust, they are usually referring to the almost complete destruction of Europe's Jews by Nazi Germany. Jews from all over German-occupied Europe were sent to special prisons called **concentration camps**. Some were work camps where prisoners were worked to death. Others were death camps where prisoners were killed. Other people whom the Nazis considered "unfit"—such as gypsies, communists, the mentally or physically handicapped, and political opponents—were also killed. From 1941 to the end of the war in 1945, more than twelve million prisoners were murdered in the camps. Six million of them were Jews.

Dwight David Eisenhower

WAR HERO

Dwight David Eisenhower (1890–1969) was called to the United States War Department as a Philippines expert shortly after Japan's attack on Pearl Harbor. In 1942, he was given command of U.S. forces in Europe by Army Chief of Staff **George C. Marshall**. By 1944, Eisenhower was a full general; as supreme commander of all Allied forces, he supervised the preparation of air, sea, and land forces for the invasion of Normandy (D-Day). After the war, as army chief of staff, he was in charge of demobilizing the wartime army while at the same time assuring a suitable peacetime defense force. Eisenhower was a popular war hero. He ran for president in 1952 and defeated his Democratic opponent, **Adlai Stevenson**.

American battle deaths in World War II numbered 405,399. There were few American civilian casualties. Worldwide, however, casualties (including military and civilian deaths) totaled approximately 55 million.

ECONOMIC BOOM

After the war (from 1945 until approximately 1973), there was an economic boom in the United States, Japan, and Western Europe. People were eager to buy things that had not been available during the war, and factories—no longer turning out goods for the war effort—were able to concentrate on filling consumer orders. A huge amount of financial aid from the United States to Western Europe and Japan fueled a rebuilding boom in those countries. Cheap and plentiful fuel and the investment in the rest of the world by multi-national companies also contributed to the boom.

THE UNITED NATIONS

U.S. President **Franklin D. Roosevelt**, Prime Minister **Winston Churchill** of Great Britain, and Soviet Premier **Joseph Stalin** were known as the "Big Three." Before the end of the war, they discussed forming an organization that would encourage peace in the world. Together, they worked out the details for what became the **United Nations** (U.N.). Fifty nations signed the original U.N. charter in 1945. There are now 185 members. The U.N. is headquartered in New York City.

UNITED NATIONS' STRUCTURE

The **General Assembly** is made up of all U.N. member nations. It can discuss any issue important to the world. Each country has one vote. The General Assembly sets the United Nations' budget, admits new members, and appoints the secretary-general.

The **Security Council** discusses questions of peace and security. It is composed of fifteen members. The five permanent members—China, France, Great Britain, Russia, and the United States—are known as the great powers. A "no" vote, known as veto power, from any permanent member can defeat a resolution.

The **Secretariat** is the administrative, or management, arm of the United Nations. It is headed by a secretary-general, who serves a five-year term. He or she appoints the U.N. staff to carry out the organization's day-to-day business.

The United Nations Building

COLD WAR

The period of rivalry and mistrust between the United States and the Soviet Union after World War II is called the **Cold War**. Each side, wanting to be stronger than the other, continued building more powerful weapons of mass destruction. In 1989, the **Berlin Wall** (a wall that had separated East and West Germany) was dismantled and Germany was reunited. This symbolized the beginning of a process to end the Cold War.

NATO AND THE WARSAW PACT

In 1949, the **North Atlantic Treaty Organization (NATO)** was formed by the United States, Canada, and free nations of Western Europe. Its goal was to limit the spread of communism and to defend democratic nations from attack. In 1955, the Soviet Union and seven communist countries of Eastern Europe formed the **Warsaw Pact**, also with the purpose of defending one another from attacks. In 1991, the Warsaw Pact was dissolved.

KOREAN WAR (1950–1953)

After World War II, Korea was divided into two parts. North Korea had a Soviet-supported communist government. South Korea had an anticommunist government supported by the United States. In an attempt to unite the country by force, North Korea attacked the South. United Nations forces and U.S. troops defended South Korea. After three years of war, a truce was declared, but the country remained divided.

Who were the Big Three? Write your answer on the flap.

VIETNAM WAR

Which five nations are permanent members of the U.N. Security Council? Write your answer on the flap.

There is no formal start date for the Vietnam War, but U.S. involvement in the conflict gradually increased from 1950 until 1973. Before World War II, Vietnam had been a French colony. After the war, Vietnam was split—the North became communist, and the South noncommunist. Many U.S. presidents, beginning with Truman, aided the South. The Communist government in Hanoi, however, was determined to reunify the country. In 1960, North Vietnam announced its intention "to liberate South Vietnam from the ruling yoke of the U.S. imperialists and their henchmen." By 1969, America had 543,400 troops in Vietnam. But as U.S. military involvement grew, a peace movement developed at home. During the late 1960s and early 1970s, antiwar protesters became more and more outspoken. They organized marches in major cities and demonstrated on many college campuses across the country. In Ohio, at Kent State University, National Guard troops fired into a crowd of protesters, killing four students and injuring nine.

What does NATO stand for? Write your answer on the flap.

President Nixon's special adviser **Henry Kissinger** and North Vietnamese representative **Le Duc Tho** were able to agree to terms for a cease-fire on January 28, 1973. At the time of the cease-fire, 587 U.S. military personnel and civilian POW's were returned; approximately 2,500 prisoners of war were unaccounted for. Nearly 60,000 Americans had been killed in the war and 153,000 wounded. On April 30, 1975, South Vietnam fell to the communists, who also gained control of neighboring Cambodia and Laos.

John Fitzgerald Kennedy: In 1961, at the age of forty-three, John Fitzgerald Kennedy became the country's youngest elected president. Kennedy inspired ordinary people to serve their country through volunteer programs such as the Peace Corps. His promise to send an American to the moon excited the whole country. The nation was shocked when an assassin's bullet tragically ended Kennedy's life on November 22, 1963.

Lyndon Baines Johnson: After Kennedy's assassination Lyndon B. Johnson became president. In 1964, he was elected to his own term as president. Johnson created programs for social reforms and major civil rights legislation, known as the **Great Society**. Programs were created to fight poverty and to improve the quality of American life. This was called Johnson's "war on poverty." Congress implemented 226 of Johnson's 252 legislative requests during his term in office. But Johnson's expansion of U.S. involvement in Vietnam turned many Americans against him. By 1967, he had to avoid public appearances because of demonstrations and threats on his life. On March 31, 1968, in an effort to heal the divisions in the country, Johnson announced in a televised speech: "I shall not seek, and I will not accept, the nomination of my party for another term as your president." In May of that year, he initiated peace talks in Paris between U.S. and North Vietnamese representatives.

Richard Nixon: After losing the race for president in 1960 and a bid for governor of California in 1962, Richard Nixon made a remarkable comeback and in 1968 was elected president of the United States. He had many successes in domestic and foreign affairs, including opening relations with China and the Soviet Union and ending U.S. participation in the Vietnam war. However, his name will always be linked with a scandal called **Watergate**. The Democratic National Committee headquarters were in the Watergate, an apartment building in Washington, D.C. In 1972, the offices were burglarized by people who worked for the committee to reelect Nixon (for a second term as president). Though it is believed that Nixon had no advance knowledge of the break-in, he interfered with an investigation of the crime. Facing impeachment by the House of Representatives, he resigned from office on August 9, 1974. He was later pardoned by President Gerald Ford.

Mikhail Gorbachev: General secretary of the Communist Party and president of the Soviet Union, Mikhail Gorbachev initiated reforms that helped to end the Cold War. Between 1985 and 1990, he introduced *perestroika*—a series of steps to restructure Soviet society. He encouraged *glasnost*, an openness in political and cultural affairs. When the Soviet Union voted itself out of existence on December 25, 1991, Gorbachev resigned as president.

John Fitzgerald Kennedy

Lyndon Johnson

Richard Nixon

THE SPACE PROGRAM

Lunar Module

THE SPACE PROGRAM

After the Soviet Union launched a satellite, *Sputnik I*, on October 4, 1957, the race to space was on between the United States and the USSR. The Soviets were first again when, on April 12, 1961, Yuri Gagarin became the first human in space. Also in 1961, Alan Shepard became the first American in space. On February 20, 1962, John Glenn became the first American to orbit the earth. On July 20, 1969, Neil Armstrong and Edwin Aldrin, flying on the spaceship *Apollo 11*, became the first humans to walk on the moon. A tragic blow to the U.S. space program was the explosion on January 28, 1986, of the space shuttle *Challenger* along with its crew of seven. One of the mission specialists, a civilian named Christa McAuliffe, was to be the first teacher in space. Though the goal of landing a man on the moon was achieved, no permanent lunar base has yet been established. On October 29, 1998, aboard the shuttle *Discovery*, seventy-seven-year-old Senator John Glenn, the same man who orbited the earth in 1962, became the oldest person to go into space.

HIGHLIGHTS: RECENT U.S. HISTORY

1976 The United States celebrates the Bicentennial, its two-hundredth birthday.

1981 Sandra Day O'Connor becomes the first female justice on the Supreme Court.

1983 Martin Luther King, Jr.'s birthday is declared a national holiday.

1987 The stock market plunges 508 points, but the economy stabilizes.

1989 General Colin Powell becomes the first African-American chairman of the Joint Chiefs of Staff, the senior members of each branch of the military.

1991 The Persian Gulf War (also called Operation Desert Storm) is fought to force Iraq to withdraw its forces from neighboring Kuwait. Under the command of General Norman Schwarzkopf, Kuwait is liberated in a war lasting one hundred hours.

1993 The North American Free Trade Agreement (NAFTA) is signed into law. NAFTA ends trade barriers among the United States, Canada, and Mexico.

1998-1999 The House of Representatives votes for impeachment of President William J. Clinton. The Senate votes against conviction and President Clinton is exonerated.

CHAPTER 10

Civil Rights

LANDMARK CASE

Earl Warren, the fourteenth Chief Justice of the Supreme Court, led the court in making important changes in civil rights laws. One of the most significant victories for civil rights was **Brown vs. Board of Education of Topeka**. This landmark civil rights case, decided by Warren's court in 1954, ruled that segregation in public schools was unconstitutional. Warren wrote that "separate educational facilities are inherently unequal" and ordered that schools be desegregated "with all deliberate speed."

Even so, many states resisted the ruling. In 1957, President Eisenhower had to send federal troops to Little Rock, Arkansas, to protect black students who were attempting to attend a formerly all-white school. By the early 1980s, still only eighty percent of the schools in the South were integrated.

LEADERS AND ORGANIZATIONS

In 1955, **Rosa Parks**, known as the "mother of the civil rights struggle," was arrested for violating segregation laws in Montgomery, Alabama. She refused to give up her seat on a bus to a white person. To protest this discrimination, the Reverend **Martin Luther King, Jr.**, arranged a boycott of the Montgomery bus system. The boycott lasted for 381 days and resulted in a repeal of the law. In June 1999 Rosa Parks was awarded the Congressional Gold Medal, the highest civilian honor given by the United States.

Martin Luther King, Jr. (1929–1968), emerged as a leader of the civil rights movement after organizing the Montgomery bus boycott. A respected clergyman, Nobel laureate, and powerful speaker, King believed in using nonviolent tactics to achieve equal rights for blacks. His famous "I Have a Dream" speech was delivered during the civil rights march on Washington, D.C., in 1963. Dr. King was assassinated in Memphis, Tennessee, on April 4, 1968.

Martin Luther King, Jr.

LEADERS AND ORGANIZATIONS

As a young man, **Malcolm X** (1925–1965) became interested in the teachings of Elijah Muhammad, a leader of the Black Muslims (also known as the Nation of Islam). The Muslims believed in racial separation, and Malcolm became their most important spokesman. In 1964, Malcolm formed the **Organization of Afro-American Unity (OAAU)**, following a pilgrimage to the Islamic holy city of Mecca. After further travels to Africa and Europe, Malcolm took the Arabic name of El-Hajj Malik El-Shabazz and began preaching racial solidarity. On February 21, 1965, Malcolm was assassinated by men associated with the Black Muslims.

March on Washington, D.C.

CIVIL RIGHTS ACT OF 1964

On August 28, 1963, more than two hundred thousand people marched on Washington, D.C., to support the civil rights bill. When President Lyndon Johnson signed the Civil Rights Act of 1964, discrimination based on race or color in the workplace, public facilities, unions, housing, and federally funded programs became illegal.

State*	Date of Admission	Capital	Population**
Alabama	December 14, 1819	Montgomery	4,319,154
Alaska	January 3, 1959	Juneau	609,311
Arizona	February 14, 1912	Phoenix	4,554,966
Arkansas	June 15, 1836	Little Rock	2,522,819
California	September 9, 1850	Sacramento	32,268,301
Colorado	August 1, 1876	Denver	3,392,644
Connecticut	January 9, 1788	Hartford	3,269,858
Delaware	December 7, 1787	Dover	731,581
Florida	March 3, 1845	Tallahassee	14,653,945
Georgia	January 2, 1788	Atlanta	7,486,242
Hawaii	August 21, 1959	Honolulu	1,186,602
Idaho	July 3, 1890	Boise	1,210,232
Illinois	December 3, 1818	Springfield	11,895,849
Indiana	December 11, 1816	Indianapolis	5,864,108
Iowa	December 28, 1846	Des Moines	2,852,423
Kansas	January 29, 1861	Topeka	2,594,840
Kentucky	June 1, 1792	Frankfort	3,908,124
Louisiana	April 30, 1812	Baton Rouge	4,351,769
Maine	March 15, 1820	Augusta	1,242,051
Maryland	April 28, 1788	Annapolis	5,094,289
Massachusetts	February 6, 1788	Boston	6,117,520
Michigan	January 26, 1837	Lansing	9,773,892
Minnesota	May 11, 1858	St. Paul	4,685,549
Mississippi	December 10, 1817	Jackson	2,730,501
Missouri	August 10, 1821	Jefferson City	5,402,058
Montana	November 8, 1889	Helena	878,810
Nebraska	March 1, 1867	Lincoln	1,656,870
Nevada	October 31, 1864	Carson City	1,676,809
New Hampshire	June 21, 1788	Concord	1,172,709
New Jersey	December 18, 1787	Trenton	8,052,849
New Mexico	January 6, 1912	Santa Fe	1,729,751
New York	July 26, 1788	Albany	18,137,226
North Carolina	November 21, 1789	Raleigh	6,733,996
North Dakota	November 2, 1889	Bismarck	640,883
Ohio	March 1, 1803	Columbus	11,186,331
Oklahoma	November 16, 1907	Oklahoma City	3,317,091
Oregon	February 14, 1859	Salem	3,243,487
Pennsylvania	December 12, 1787	Harrisburg	12,019,661
Rhode Island	May 29, 1790	Providence	987,429
South Carolina	May 23, 1788	Columbia	3,760,181
South Dakota	November 2, 1889	Pierre	737,973
Tennessee	June 1, 1796	Nashville	5,368,198
Texas	December 29, 1845	Austin	19,439,337
Utah	January 4, 1896	Salt Lake City	2,059,148
Vermont	March 4, 1791	Montpelier	588,978
Virginia	June 25, 1788	Richmond	7,425,183
Washington	November 11, 1889	Olympia	5,610,362
West Virginia	June 20, 1863	Charleston	1,815,787
Wisconsin	May 29, 1848	Madison	5,169,677
Wyoming	July 10, 1890	Cheyenne	479,743

* Puerto Rico became a self-governing commonwealth in 1952.
 Its capital city is San Juan, and population is 3,522,000.
** based on *The World Almanac for Kids 1999*, World Almanac Book, Primedia Co., 1998.

No.	Name	Term*	Political Party	Vice President
1	George Washington	1789–1797	None	John Adams
2	John Adams	1797–1801	Federalist	Thomas Jefferson
3	Thomas Jefferson	1801–1809	Dem./Republican**	Aaron Burr, George Clinton
4	James Madison	1809–1817	Dem./Republican	George Clinton, Elbridge Gerry
5	James Monroe	1817–1825	Dem./Republican	Daniel D. Tompkins
6	John Quincy Adams	1825–1829	Dem./Republican	John C. Calhoun
7	Andrew Jackson	1829–1837	Democratic	John C. Calhoun, Martin Van Buren
8	Martin Van Buren	1837–1841	Democratic	Richard M. Johnson
9	William Henry Harrison	1841	Whig	John Tyler
10	John Tyler	1841–1845	Whig	——
11	James K. Polk	1845–1849	Democratic	George M. Dallas
12	Zachary Taylor	1849–1850	Whig	Millard Fillmore
13	Millard Fillmore	1850–1853	Whig	——
14	Franklin Pierce	1853–1857	Democratic	William R. King†
15	James Buchanan	1857–1861	Democratic	John C. Breckinridge
16	Abraham Lincoln	1861–1865	Republican	Hannibal Hamlin Andrew Johnson
17	Andrew Johnson	1865–1869	Democratic	——
18	Ulysses S. Grant	1869–1877	Republican	Schuyler Colfax, Henry Wilson
19	Rutherford B. Hayes	1877–1881	Republican	William A. Wheeler
20	James A. Garfield	1881	Republican	Chester A. Arthur
21	Chester A. Arthur	1881–1885	Republican	——
22	Grover Cleveland	1885–1889	Democratic	Thomas A. Hendricks
23	Benjamin Harrison	1889–1893	Republican	Levi P. Morton
24	Grover Cleveland	1893–1897	Democratic	Adlai E. Stevenson
25	William McKinley	1897–1901	Republican	Garret A. Hobart Theodore Roosevelt
26	Theodore Roosevelt	1901–1909	Republican	Charles W. Fairbanks
27	William Howard Taft	1909–1913	Republican	James S. Sherman
28	Woodrow Wilson	1913–1921	Democratic	Thomas R. Marshall
29	Warren G. Harding	1921–1923	Republican	Calvin Coolidge
30	Calvin Coolidge	1923–1929	Republican	Charles G. Dawes
31	Herbert C. Hoover	1929–1933	Republican	Charles Curtis
32	Franklin D. Roosevelt	1933–1945	Democratic	John Nance Garner, Henry A. Wallace, Harry S. Truman
33	Harry S. Truman	1945–1953	Democratic	Alben W. Barkley (1949–1953)
34	Dwight D. Eisenhower	1953–1961	Republican	Richard M. Nixon
35	John F. Kennedy	1961–1963	Democratic	Lyndon B. Johnson
36	Lyndon B. Johnson	1963–1969	Democratic	Hubert H. Humphrey††
37	Richard M. Nixon	1969–1974	Republican	Spiro T. Agnew, Gerald R. Ford
38	Gerald R. Ford	1974–1977	Republican	Nelson A. Rockefeller
39	James E. Carter	1977–1981	Democratic	Walter F. Mondale
40	Ronald W. Reagan	1981–1989	Republican	George H. W. Bush
41	George H. W. Bush	1989–1993	Republican	J. Danforth Quayle
42	William J. Clinton	1993–	Democratic	Albert Gore

* Terms are dated from the inauguration, not from the election.
** The Democratic-Republican party of the third through sixth presidents was not the same as the modern Republican party, which was founded in 1854.
† Died in office (1853)
†† Elected term only (1965–1969)

John Tyler, Millard Fillmore, Andrew Johnson, and Chester A. Arthur became president after their predecessors died in office. Therefore, they did not have vice presidents. Both Harry S. Truman and Lyndon B. Johnson became president after the deaths of the sitting president. For the duration of these terms the office of vice president was vacant. In 1967, the Twenty-fifth Amendment provided that "whenever there is a vacancy in the office of the Vice president, the President shall nominate a vice president."

INDEX

INDEX

H

Hale, Nathan, 17
Hamilton, Alexander, 17
Hayes, Rutherford B., 38
Henry, Patrick, 17
Hiroshima (Japan), bombing of, 51
Hitler, Adolf, 49, 51
Holocaust, 52
Homestead Act (1862), 25
Hoover, Herbert, 46
House of Burgesses, 9, 17
House of Representatives, 21, 22, 23, 55
Houston, Sam, 28

I

immigration, 41
Indian Removal Act (1830), 30
Indians, 7. *See also* Native Americans
Industrial Revolution, 39–41
Intolerable Acts, 15
inventions and inventors, 17, 40
Italy, 43, 44, 50, 51

J

Jackson, Andrew, 30
Jamestown colony, 9
Japan, 49, 50, 51, 52
Jefferson, Thomas
    Declaration of Independence, 16
    Louisiana Purchase, 26
    president, 26
    Secretary of State, 17
Jim Crow laws, 38
Johnson, Andrew, 38
Johnson, Lyndon Baines, 55, 58
Jolliet, Louis, 8
Jones, John Paul, 17

K

Kansas, 32, 46
Kennedy, John Fitzgerald, 55
Kentucky, 25
Key, Francis Scott, 24
King, Martin Luther, Jr., 56, 57
Kissinger, Henry, 54
Korean War, 54
Ku Klux Klan (KKK), 38

L

labor unions, 41
    goals of, 41
Lafayette, Marquis de, 17
land bridge, 5
La Salle, René-Robert, 8
League of Nations, 45
Le Duc Tho, 54
Lee, Robert E., 36, 37
Lewis and Clark expedition (1804), 25, 26, 27
Lewis, John L., 41
Lewis, Meriwether, 26

Lexington, Massachusetts, 14, 15
Liberator, The (abolitionist newspaper), 32
Lincoln, Abraham, 32, 33, 36, 37
    assassination, 37
    Civil War, 33, 36
Lincoln-Douglas debates (1858), 32
Livingston, Robert, 16
Louis XIV (king of France), 8
Louisiana Purchase (1803), 25, 26, 31
Lusitania, 43

M

Madison, James, 19, 26
Maine, 31
Maine, 42
Malcolm X, 58
Mandan Indians, 26
manifest destiny, 24, 25, 28
Marquette, Jacques, 8
Marshall, George C., 50, 52
Marshall Plan, 50
Maryland, 10, 32
Massachusetts, 9, 10, 14, 15, 32
    American Revolution, 14, 15
    Shays' Rebellion, 19
Mayflower, 9
Mayflower Compact, 9
McClellan, George, 36
Meany, George, 41
Mexican Cession, 31
Mexican War (1846–1848), 25, 28, 36
    causes, 28
    results, 28
Mexico, 28
Middle Passage, 12
minutemen, 15
Mississippi River, 8, 14, 16, 25, 26
Mississippi Valley, 14
Missouri, 26, 29, 31, 32
Missouri Compromise (1820), 31
Monroe Doctrine, 24
Monroe, James, 24
monopoly, 40
Mott, Lucretia Coffin, 45

N

Nagasaki (Japan), bombing of, 51
Napoleon, 26
National Association for the Advancement of Colored People (NAACP), 38
nationalism, 43
National Labor Relations Act (NLRA), 48
National Recovery Act (NRA), 48
National Socialist German Workers' Party (Nazi), 49, 52
Nation of Islam, 58
Native Americans, 5, 6, 7, 8, 9, 13, 14, 15, 24, 26, 29, 30. *See also* westward expansion.
    culture groups (tribes), 5, 6, 30
    resettlement of, 30
    Trail of Tears, 30

New Deal, 47–48
New France territory, 8, 13
New Mexico, 28, 31
New Orleans, 14, 26
New World, 7, 9
New York, 10, 12, 32, 45
Nineteenth Amendment, 45
Nixon, Richard, 54, 55
North America, 5, 7, 9, 12, 14, 16, 24
North American Free Trade Agreement (NAFTA), 56
North Atlantic Treaty Organization (NATO), 54
North Star (antislavery newspaper), 32
Northwest Ordinance (1787), 25, 26
Northwest Territory, 26

O

order of power in U.S. government, 22
Oregon Trail, 25
Organization of Afro-American Unity, 58
overland routes, 25. *See also* westward expansion.

P

Paine, Thomas, 17
Parks, Rosa, 57
Parliament, British, 15
Pearl Harbor, 49, 51, 52
Pennsylvania, 10, 14
Pennsylvania, University of, 17
Perry, Admiral Oliver Hazard, 24
Persian Gulf War, 56
Philadelphia, 12, 15, 17, 19, 22
    Continental Congress, 15
Philippines, U.S. acquisition of, 42
picketing (labor unions), 41
Pilgrims, 9, 10, 11
pioneers, 25-26
Pitt, William, 13
plantations, 12
Plymouth colony, 9, 10
Pocahontas, 9
Polk, James K., 28
Pony Express, 29
popular sovereignty, 20
Portugal, 7, 8
post-war regression, 38
Powell, Colin, 56
Powhatan, 9
prairie schooner, 29
presidency, the, 21–23, 60
    checks and balances, 21
    order of succession, 22
    president as chief executive, 21
    veto power, 23
principles of government, 20
Proclamation of 1763, 15
Public Works Administration (PWA), 48
Puerto Rico, U.S. acquisition of, 42
Puritans, 10, 11, 12

PAGE 7
Native Americans; from Asia

PAGE 8
Vasco de Balboa

PAGE 9
1. representative government
2. Sir Walter Raleigh

PAGE 11
two

PAGE 12
New York, Delaware, New Jersey, Pennsylvania

PAGE 17
Thomas Jefferson, Benjamin Franklin, John Adams, Roger Sherman, Robert Livingston

PAGE 18
Alexander Hamilton

PAGE 20
1. Articles of Confederation
2. executive, legislative, judicial

PAGE 22
legislative

PAGE 23
Bill of Rights; protect rights of individuals

PAGE 24
if two-thirds of Congress votes for it

PAGE 26
1. Wilderness Road
2. Illinois, Indiana, Michigan, Ohio, and Wisconsin

PAGE 28
continental divide

PAGE 30
1. gold miners who went to California in 1849
2. Promontory, Utah

PAGE 34
1. attack on Fort Sumter by Confederates
2. South Carolina

PAGE 35
Jefferson Davis

PAGE 37
Merrimack and *Monitor*

PAGE 38
1. Reconstruction
2. Fourteenth

PAGE 41
monopoly

PAGE 42
1. American Federation of Labor; Samuel Gompers
2. strike

PAGE 44
assassination of Archduke Francis Ferdinand

PAGE 45
France, Great Britain, Italy, Russia, United States, Serbia

PAGE 46
League of Nations

PAGE 47
a period of low production and sales, plus high rates of business failures and unemployment

PAGE 50
Dec. 7, 1941; "a date that will live in infamy"

PAGE 51
to help rebuild Europe

PAGE 54
1. Roosevelt, Churchill, Stalin
2. China, France, Great Britain, Russia, United States
3. North Atlantic Treaty Organization